A Boomer's Guide to Grandparenting

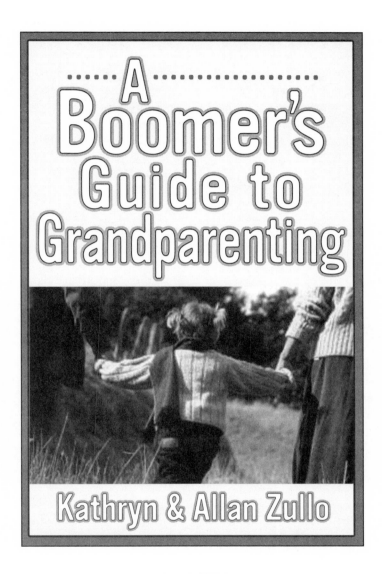

A Boomer's Guide to Grandparenting

Kathryn & Allan Zullo

Revised Edition

**Andrews McMeel
Publishing**

Kansas City

04 05 06 07 08 FFG 10 9 8 7 6 5 4 3 2 1

Library of Congress Cataloging-in-Publication Data

Zullo, Kathryn.
    A boomer's guide to grandparenting / Kathryn and Allan Zullo.—
Rev. ed.
        p.   cm.
    Rev. ed. of: The nanas and the papas : a boomer's guide to grandparenting /
Kathryn and Allan Zullo. 1998.
    ISBN 0-7407-4749-5
    1. Grandparenting—United States. 2. Baby boom generation—United
States. 3. Grandparents—United States—Family relationships. 4.
Grandparent and child—United States. I. Zullo, Allan. II. Zullo,
Kathryn. Nanas and the papas. 1998 III. Title.

HQ759.9.Z85 2004
306.874'5—dc22

2004047689

Book design by Pete Lippincott

ATTENTION: SCHOOLS AND BUSINESSES

Andrews McMeel books are available at quantity discounts with bulk purchase for educational, business, or sales promotional use. For information, please write to: Special Sales Department, Andrews McMeel Publishing, 4520 Main Street, Kansas City, Missouri 64111.

This is dedicated to the ones we love—

our grandsons Chad Alexander and Danny Allan
and (hopefully) any future grandchildren.

Contents

Acknowledgments

WE ARE EXTREMELY GRATEFUL for the assistance of all the experts who shared with us their research, comments, and advice.

This book could not have been completed without the cooperation, understanding, and encouragement of the guru of grandparents, Arthur Kornhaber, M.D., founder of the Foundation for Grandparenting.

We also wish to thank the following experts for providing us with much needed and valued information: Barbara Bowman, president of the Erikson Institute; T. Berry Brazelton, M.D., noted author and pediatrician; Perry Buffington, Ph.D., psychologist and host of his own syndicated radio show; Susan Ginsberg, Ed.D., editor and publisher of *Work & Family Life*; Amy Goyer, coordinator of the AARP Grandparent Information Center; Anya Luchow Liberman, Ph.D., psychologist and family mediator; Jody Martin, curriculum specialist for the Children's World Learning Center; Peter Martin, Ph.D., professor of human development and family studies at Iowa State University; Susan Newman, Ph.D., sociologist and author; Gregory F. Sanders, Ph.D., associate professor of child development and family relations at North Dakota State University; attorney Richard Victor, executive director of the Grandparents Rights Organization; and Jeffrey Wallem, CFP, of Wallem Associates.

In addition, we appreciate the help of the following: Pat Connolly, Jane Curry, David Fenech, Whitney Gilman, Jay Goodman, Danny Manausa, Nita Marlow, John McLain, and Martha Moffett.

We especially want to thank all the nanas and papas who took the time to share with us their thoughts, experiences, and suggestions.

Sunshine, Lollipops, and Rainbows

Introduction

"Mom, Dad," said our daughter Allison on the speakerphone. "How would you like to be called by different names?"

"Like what?" we asked. "The Captain and Tennille?"

"No," Allison replied, "something more along the lines of" . . . she paused for dramatic effect . . . "Nana and Papa."

"Oh, my God!" we roared. "You're pregnant!"

"Yes, you're going to be grandparents!"

Thrilled by the news, we happily pictured all the fun we would have with our first grandchild—showering him with love, plying him with forbidden treats behind his parents' backs, taking him hiking and canoeing, and buying him the hippest clothes. (We assumed it would be a boy because our son-in-law Dan came from a family of five boys.)

But then we experienced a slight moment of panic. What did we really know about being grandparents? It was in the fall of 1995. We were active fortysomethings—nothing like the stereotypical gray-haired grandmas and grandpas who sat in rocking chairs, baked cookies, whittled toys, and told stories of the "good old days." We weren't like the Ensure-swilling senior citizens or the frumpy, wrinkled elderly neighbors so often portrayed in TV commercials and movies.

Kathryn (reminiscing about her childhood visits with her grandmother Melba): *"I would wake up in my grandparents' farmhouse to the smell of fresh cinnamon rolls baking in the oven. In the afternoon I'd find a batch of Grandma's homemade cookies cooling on the rack. She made bread from scratch and picked vegetables from her garden. After a week at Grandma's, I would go home with a sweater that she had knit by hand. She had twenty-six* *grandchildren—and she made every one of them sweaters when they came to visit.*

"I adored my grandmother. I always thought everyone should have a grandma like mine. But I can't be like her. I don't bake cookies. I don't knit sweaters. I don't grow my own veggies. I don't have time, with all the work and travel I do. What kind of a grandmother is that?"

Allan: *"My grandparents died before I was old enough to remember them. My role models were fashioned from TV—a cross between Grandpa McCoy and Grandpa Munster."*

We were typical boomer grandparents-to-be—younger, healthier, wealthier, and better educated than our grandparents were. We were more active and less formal than our own parents were at our age. We no longer fit the traditional yet unrealistic image of our elderly kin because they lived in a different period.

We were determined to become the best grandparents possible by relying on our heart, our instincts, and the confidence that we'd do a good job. But life, families, and roles are so different now than when our grandparents and parents were tending to their grandkids. Hoping to get a little guidance, we headed to the bookstores shortly after our grandson Chad was born. We searched for a book on grandparenting aimed at our generation, a guide that would offer tips and suggestions helpful to us.

We found several fine books written by experts. But they dealt with older grandparents who had time on their hands. Almost all the books were warmhearted memoirs, detailed studies, or straight how-to's for the retired grandparent. Although many of the experts' tips certainly made sense for nanas and papas of any age and any generation, we still couldn't find a book that spoke directly to us—boomer grandparents.

How does the boomer cope with the changing dynamics of today's family? Deal with new parenting techniques and baby products? Spend quality time with the grandkids while still pursuing work and enjoying pastimes?

That's when we decided to write *The Nanas and the Papas,* a book geared toward expectant boomer grandparents and those with infant or toddler grandkids. For the book, we sought out experts who offered relevant tips, suggestions, experiences, and the latest research that has the greatest impact on new grandparents.

We interviewed the guru of grandparents, Arthur Kornhaber, M.D., founder of the Foundation for Grandparenting. He and his wife Carol initiated the Grandparent Study to systematically investigate the grandparent/grandchild relationship, research that continues to this day. Dr. Kornhaber, a grandpa who since 1970 has been a tireless champion for grandparent involvement in family life, graciously answered our questions and allowed us to quote from his studies.

We also interviewed grandmother and respected educator Barbara Bowman, president of the Chicago-based Erikson Institute for the Advanced Study of Child Development, which is a private graduate school and research center; T. Berry Brazelton, M.D., the internationally-renowned pediatrician, author of *Touchpoints: Your Child's Emotional and Behavioral Development*, founder of the Child Development Unit of Children's Hospital in Boston, cofounder of the national advocacy group Parent Action, and a grandfather; Perry (Doctor Buff) Buffington, Ph.D., a fellow boomer and noted family psychologist with his own syndicated radio show; Susan Ginsberg, Ed.D., editor and publisher of the national newsletter *Work & Family Life* and a grandmother; Jody Martin, curriculum specialist for the Children's World Learning Center, a nationwide child care provider; Peter Martin, Ph.D., professor of human development and family studies at Iowa State University and a fellow boomer; Susan Newman, Ph.D., sociologist, author, and grandmother; Gregory F. Sanders, Ph.D., associate professor of child development and family relations at North Dakota State University; and attorney Richard Victor, executive director of the Grandparents Rights Organization.

In addition, we gathered informative and wry observations, advice, and accounts from other boomer grandparents through personal interviews, e-mail, and various grandparent and boomer Web sites. Their comments, in italics, are scattered throughout the book. In most cases, we used their real names or their e-mail nicknames. But in a few sensitive cases, some names were changed to protect their identity. (Comments labeled from Kathryn or Allan are from us, the authors.)

The book was originally published in the fall of 1998, four months after the birth of our second grandson Danny. We were gratified by the nationwide attention the book received. We were interviewed countless times on radio and for various publications and appeared on the *Today Show* and National Public Radio. But by the fall of 2003, we realized that the landscape for grandparents had changed just enough—with developments such as the Supreme Court's ruling on visitation rights, changes in tax laws for grandchildren's college funds, and increases in the number of stepgrandparents and grandparents raising grandchildren—that we felt it was time to come out with a new edition.

So we went back to the experts and asked them more questions. This edition reflects their answers and insights as well as the results of the latest grandparent studies that weren't available at the time the first edition was published. We also interviewed boomer grandmom and psychologist Anya Luchow Liberman, Ph.D., an adviser for grandparents.com for her thoughts. We've included comments from new boomer grandparents and their adult children as well as veteran boomer nanas and papas who spoke with us for the first book. In addition, we've updated a section in the back with resources that might prove helpful. It includes Web sites, e-mail and snail-mail addresses, and phone numbers of grandparenting organizations, support groups, and newsletters, as well as recommended reading.

The same issues that we explored in our first edition are even more prevalent today. Many boomer grandparents work hard and lead vigorous, often stressful, lives where time is a valuable commodity. We must deal with issues far removed from what our grandparents faced. Our adult children's ideas of child-rearing is often very different from the views of Dr. Spock, to whom we once pledged allegiance. Millions of boomers must help raise the grandkids because of economic pressures or personal problems of their adult children. Other factors, such as living in far-flung communities and coping with divorce, make it more of a challenge for boomers to play a meaningful part in our grandchildren's lives.

For way too many kids, the family life typified by the Cleavers, Stones, and Andersons can be experienced only on Nick at Nite. An analysis by the Population Reference Bureau in 2003 revealed that just

36 percent of all families in the United States are considered tradi-tional, where Mom and Dad preside over the nuclear brood. In fact, if Ward, Jim, and Alex and their stay-at-home wives were raising the kids today, families like them, where Dad is the sole breadwinner, would represent only 13 percent of all married-couple households.

When we were kids, new friends asked each other, "What does your father do for a living?" Now the question asked is, "Does your dad live with you?" Children are far more likely to live with a never-married mother than we boomers ever were. Eleven percent of today's kids—nearly eight million—live with one parent who has never married and another 15 percent, or about eleven million, are being raised by a divorced, single parent. An even larger share of U.S. children, about 40 percent, will live with their unmarried mother and her boyfriend sometime before their sixteenth birthday, according to a study sup-ported by the National Institute of Child Health and Human Development.

We have too many families that are blended and broken, strained and strapped. In increasing numbers, adult children who are drugged-out, wiped-out, or stressed-out have shown up on their parents' doorstep and said, "Here, take care of my kids." Over 6 percent of all children today, about 4.5 million, are living in their grandparents' home, according to the U.S. Census Bureau.

And there's another challenge facing today's boomer grandparents. For the first time in history, a generation of grandparents will be caring for their parents. We boomers must find ways to handle our lives while providing help for our elderly parents as well as for our adult children and grandchildren.

Child-rearing has changed so much since we raised our kids. There are new rules about what to do and not to do. That old crib you saved for the day you became a grandparent must be thrown out because the rails are too far apart. The baby quilt you wanted to hand down is a no-no, at least until the child is much older. That old windup swing with the chains? Throw it away. The baby's fingers can get caught in the mechanism.

There's so much to learn (and unlearn) now: Don't put the baby on her tummy for a nap, Nana; put her on her back. Toss out the baby aspirin, Papa; use children's ibuprofen instead. No, Grammy, don't give the baby any juice. It's not good for her at this age.

But some things haven't changed—like the incredible joy and unconditional love grandparents and grandchildren share. It's like sunshine, lollipops, and rainbows.

Allan: *"When Kathryn held our grandson Chad for the first time, I noticed that her teary smile and sweet murmurs mimicked those she gave our children at their births. I knew instantly she'd make a great nana.*

"When I finally wrested the baby out of her arms and cradled him in mine, I gazed at my daughter Allison and then at my father. Here together in one room was the spectrum of my life— four generations bound by blood and love. I wanted to say something profound and meaningful; words from deep within my soul; a declaration that Allison would record for posterity in Chad's baby book. I gently kissed Chad on the forehead and announced, 'Awesome!' I'll never forgive myself for such a lame remark. However, a fellow granddad consoled me by claiming that grandkids have a way of turning your mind to mush."

Now more than ever, grandparent involvement is vital to the stability and welfare of grandchildren from the moment they take their first breath. Balancing hectic lives of hard work and hard play with the needs of our grandchildren, we boomers could use a little guidance if we are to become the coolest, most understanding and loving grandparents of the twenty-first century. Through the advice of experts and the experiences of fellow boomers, we hope *A Boomer's Guide to Grandparenting* will help you enjoy to the fullest your new grand job.

Talking 'Bout Our Generation

Boomers' Newest Gig

IT'S HARD TO BELIEVE, ISN'T IT? We, the generation that defined youth—in fact, embraced it and obsessed over it—are now becoming *grandparents*.

Many of us are once again hearing the pitter-patter of little feet as the first wave of our 78-million-member generation has passed the half-century mark. Those tiny feet are multiplying into a resounding beat as more and more of our kids are having kids. Now it's our turn to grandparent. According to *Kiplinger Business Forecasts*, about 22 million, or roughly one third, of America's 70 million grandparents are boomers—people born between 1946 and 1964—and our ranks will swell to 32 million by 2007. The marketing research firm Age Wave IMPACT projects that by 2010, one out of every two grandparents will be a boomer. Because our life expectancy is increasing, we should, on average, be grandparenting longer than any previous generation, for thirty years.

Whether we like it or not, we're aging. A boomer turns fifty every seven seconds. We've gone from love beads to love handles; Volkswagen vans to minivans; rollerskates to Rollerblades. The songs we once grooved to now sell hamburgers, cars, eyeglasses, soda, and beer.

We no longer can say time is on our side. And yet it didn't seem that long ago when the pitter-patter of little feet was ours. We were the Spock babies doted on by stay-at-home moms in an era when fear was red and war was cold. We went to grade school in the shadow of the H-bomb and felt the fallout from Rosa Parks's courageous "No." We didn't know the answer to the $64,000 Question but we did to "Hey, kids, what time is it?" We fell in love with Elvis, Annette, and James. We hula-hooped and did the Twist. We were moved by Dr. King's dream and shocked by a national nightmare that stole our collective innocence one grim November day in Dallas. We flipped out over the Beatles and the Stones. We tuned in, turned on, and dropped out. We participated in be-ins, sit-ins, and love-ins. We went from the Summer of Love to the Days of Rage. We spilled our blood in Watts, Chicago, Kent State, and the jungles of Vietnam. We burned draft cards and bras. We came together on Max Yasgur's farm. We discovered Nixon was a crook and Jesus was a superstar. We were stayin' alive in discos and saying good-bye to the King of Rock. We had to imagine life without John Lennon . . . and life with Ronald Reagan. We embraced Live Aid and Farm Aid. We wept over the demise of the *Challenger* and cheered over the demise of the Berlin Wall. We began raising a generation of MTV junkies and tried to keep them from the same youthful exuberances that we had enjoyed at their age. We climbed StairMasters and corporate ladders only to watch many of us fall off later. We waged war against AIDS, crack, homelessness, and racism (arguably too little, too late). We laughed with Roseanne and with Seinfeld. We jacked up the rates of drunk driving, suicide, illegitimate births, crime, and drug use. We visited the Bridges of Madison County and rooted for Thelma and Louise. And while we sent our kids out into the real world, we put back-to-back boomers (both from the crop of '46) into the White House.

To coin a phrase from our past, what a rush!

Yet our life's journey is far from over. We boomers are now embarking on a new adventure—perhaps the most fun trip of all—as grandparents. What are we to make of this new gig? To get a clue on how we as a generation will handle this role, we need to look back at the way we were. Our history, in terms of what happened to us and what we made happen, is part of our makeup that will influence our effectiveness as family elders.

Think back. From the contented '50s to the revolutionary '60s to the restless '70s, what national event had the biggest impact on your life during your formative years? In a survey of fifty-year-old boomers conducted by *New Choices* magazine, the Vietnam War (38 percent), the assassination of John F. Kennedy (25 percent), and the social movements of the time (20 percent) were the newsmakers that affected our generation the most, shaping our values, beliefs, and attitudes.

AARP traced baby boomer attitudes in the early to mid-1970s and compared them to boomers' attitudes in 2002, and—surprise, surprise—we haven't changed our thinking very much. Back then we had shaky confidence in our government, our educational system, big business, and organized religion. Today, we still feel that way. In fact, even more so. In the '70s, 16 percent of boomers had a great deal of confidence in Congress compared to 13 percent of today's boomers; 77 percent of '70s boomers reported having only some or hardly any confidence in major corporations compared to 87 percent now; 36 percent of '70s boomers had a great deal of confidence in people running the education system compared to only 20 percent now; and, in the biggest drop of all, 30 percent of '70s boomers had confidence in organized religion compared to only 13 percent now.

"Boomers are an extremely diverse generation, extraordinarily complex yet an individualistic collection of men and women," says boomer Ken Dychtwald, president of Age Wave LLC, a market research firm. "But under the surface, we're a generation with many, many common values and experiences. We're bound together by deeply rooted values." Among the values Dychtwald lists are a belief in a meritocracy, respect for knowledge, and a lack of respect for authority.

In their enlightening book *Generations*, cultural historians William Strauss and Neil Howe say that boomers

> have morphed from Beaver Cleaver to hippie to bran-eater to yuppie to what some are calling "Neo-Puritan" in a manner quite unlike what anyone, themselves included, ever expected . . . [Boomers have] outlived any number of temporary labels: Dr. Spock, Pepsi, Rock, Now, Sixties, Love, Protest, Woodstock, Vietnam, Me, Big Chill, Yuppie and Post Yuppie Generation.
>
> From VJ Day forward, whatever age bracket Boomers have occupied has been the cultural and spiritual focal point for American society as a whole. Through their childhood, America was child-obsessed; in their youth, youth-obsessed; in their yuppie phase, yuppie-obsessed . . . Arriving as the inheritors of G.I. triumph, Boomers have always seen their mission not as constructing a society, but of justifying, even sanctifying it.

This mixture of high self-esteem and selective self-indulgence has at once repelled and fascinated other generations, giving Boomers a reputation for grating arrogance—and for transcendent cultural wisdom.

Now we're entering grandparenthood in a world far different than when our own grandmas and grandpas faced this stage of life. In the initial decade of the twenty-first century, we boomers are in our prime, earning good money, enjoying good health. We're the best-educated, most active, and youngest-looking older generation ever. Try these facts on for size: The average age of a first-time grandparent is forty-eight; the median age of a Harley Davidson owner is forty-seven.

As members of a generation that still clings to memories of its free-spirited youth, we boomers won't fade into our twilight years. We tend to think of ourselves as ten to fifteen years younger than we really are, and often act accordingly. As a result, we will shatter conventional notions of what it means to age in America, especially in a society that has coveted youth since the '60s. Because today's first-time grandparents are expected to live, on average, at least seven years longer than their grandparents, boomers are shoving back the senior years. "We're the first generation in human history that realizes that we'll be living very long lives," says Dychtwald. "So, many of us are asking, 'What's the rush?'"

AARP says nearly one in five boomers admits to actively waging war against aging. We're shelling out big bucks for the ammo, such as fitness products, skin care creams, and sexual performance-enhancing drugs. Many of us are taking more drastic actions by paying hundreds of dollars every few months to get toxic botulism injected into our faces or undergoing the knife for lifts, tucks, hair transplants, and augmentations. The American Society of Plastic Surgeons reports that since the 1980s the average age of a face-lift patient has gone from sixty to fifty.

In 2002, U.S. consumers spent more than $30 billion on antiaging products, according to the American Academy of Anti-Aging Medicine. "Hair coloring, health club memberships, personalized vitamins— boomers have opened their wallets and minds to whatever's available in this modern-day quest for the Fountain of Youth," says fellow boomer Michael J. Weiss, contributing editor of *American Demographics*. "We're youthing-down the midlife stage of our lives. My parents at age fifty would no more have thought of running a marathon than jumping off a bridge. Yet forty percent of the runners in the [2001] New York City Marathon were between forty and fifty-four years old. Boomers have always believed that getting older is for other people, like our parents, for instance. We'd prefer sex, drugs, and rock 'n' roll; you know, Elvis in his thin, younger days."

According to a 2001 survey of boomers ages forty-five to fifty-four conducted by RoperASW to determine how we feel about ourselves, we pretty much are the people we set out to be. We love to have sex (70 percent feel sexually attractive) and spend romantic evenings with our partners. Being active is a primary passion of 62 percent of boomer men and 46 percent of boomer women. Only a few of us boomers—about 10 percent—are passionate about worship. When it comes to fun, 55 percent of boomer men deliberately take time to have fun at least every few days compared to 45 percent of boomer women. A majority of us, 60 percent, constantly want to challenge ourselves with new experiences and ideas. But an overwhelming majority, 83 percent, wishes we could do more good deeds for others, and 60 percent wish our lives were more meaningful. The bottom line: As we enter our grandparenting years, we still intend to engage in a youthful, active life.

However, many of us are feeling the strain of being pulled in different directions. Our adult children need us. Our elderly parents need us. Our employers need us. Our spouses need us. Our friends need us. We worry about breast cancer and prostate cancer. We worry about money—not having enough to retire (that still seems so far away) or to maintain our current lifestyle.

"There's a lot of head-spinning going around" for boomers, says advertising veteran John Nielson, vice president of Colle & McVoy's Code 50 division, aimed at marketing to boomers. "Their fifties are a decade of enormous change, where many divorce and cope with menopause, the death of a spouse, and grandparenthood."

We have seen how downsizing, drugs, and divorce have severely stressed many families. Support systems that we took for granted when we were growing up—school, church, neighbors, and extended family—are no longer as effective in helping parents raise their children.

Now more than ever, we are realizing how vital grandparents are not only to the well-being of the family but to the well-being of the country.

So, what kind of nanas and papas will we boomers be? We might be the most self-absorbed, materialistic, spoiled generation of the previous millennium, but unless the experts are blowing smoke, we will be pretty good grandparents who likely will:

- reinvent and welcome grandparenthood
- fret over finding the time to care for our aging parents and to enjoy our grandchildren
- become conservative, caring elders
- parlay grandparenthood into a second chance at righting whatever wrongs we made as parents
- take a proactive role in helping and advising our adult children

"The boomers are not a passive generation," says Arthur Kornhaber, M.D., founder of the Foundation for Grandparenting. "They are going to say, 'I want to explore this new stage of life.' Of course, some boomers will say, 'I don't want to be old.' But I think most will want to be immortalized. And they're going to discover, 'I can immortalize myself by leaving my soul with a child.'"

Noted pediatrician T. Berry Brazelton believes we'll learn from our mistakes. "I think the baby boomers will make good grandparents," he declared.

Maureen Shea, grandmother of two: *"You know, you think you could never love anybody as much as your children, and then a grandchild comes along."*

Boomers likely will raise the consciousness of society to the important role that grandparents play. It's only natural for us boomers to alter the country's attitudes and beliefs. Call it egocentric if you want, but it's the truth. We've been doing it our whole lives.

"We have been nothing if not forceful in terms of our impact," says boomer journalist Peggy Noonan. "We are and have been the most significant demographic fact of American life in all of American history: We changed, in our youth, the culture of a great nation, sweeping it with our music, our movies, our art and styles and tastes in entertainment. Our assumptions about sex changed the sexual landscape. We altered our country's political climate when we decided to oppose a war, changing American attitudes about our government in the process."

Can there be any doubt that as our children have children we will redefine grandparenthood? We will make it up as we go along. That's been our style and we're not likely to change that. We are the hippest nanas and papas ever. "Do you realize we are going to have a generation of Grandma Heathers?" says Perry Buffington, Ph.D., a boomer and noted psychologist. "The whole image and concept of grandparents is changing."

Society may be reluctant to let go of the stereotypical picture of the gray-haired, cane-wielding grandparent, but as the number of boomer nanas and papas steadily increases, a new image will more closely reflect reality.

We will rage against age and try to make grandparenting cool, says Dr. Kornhaber "The new grandparent will have to be reinvented. We don't have any precedents for this. I have enough faith in the boomers and their ability to avoid hanging their hats on outmoded concepts of grandparenting."

Adds Peter Martin, professor of human development and family studies at Iowa State University, "Boomers by and large thought they've done a great job in affecting society since the sixties. They always believed they were fighting for a cause." Now as boomers age, we will fight to make grandparenting important, he says. "I predict boomer grandparents will define their role in more certain terms and I think they'll do a good job."

Dr. Martin, a boomer himself, believes members of our generation will be pioneers in grandparenting because we are educating ourselves about our role and how we relate to the family. "Our healthy, active lives will transmit into much stronger relationships with our grandchildren."

Glen (Pee Paw) Reed: *"My grandsons are five and three and they light up my heart like nothing else I have experienced in my forty-seven years. They beam at my approach and I beam at theirs. The love almost defies explanation and transcends time and the explanations that other relationships require."*

Although many critics claim boomers aren't, or won't be, interested in being there for their grandkids, most studies indicate that boomers, even those who cherish their independence and autonomy, want to spend as much time as possible with their grandchildren.

Phil Goodman, president and owner of Boomer Marketing Research, says that boomers want to be more of a presence in their grandchildren's everyday lives than grandparents of earlier generations were. This attitude stems partly from the fact that many boomers have fresh memories of the demands of raising children, or have kids from second or third marriages who are almost the same age as grandchildren from their first marriages. Furthermore, remembering the notorious generation gap that colored their own relations with their parents, boomers see helping with grandchildren as one way to keep communication going between them and their own children. "Boomers raised their kids to be seen and heard, but they're going to be helping their grandchildren to be seen, heard, and featured," Goodman adds.

Despite all the talk of materialism, we boomers tend to measure ourselves subjectively by the spiritual strength within. In one study, boomers were asked to compare themselves with their fathers at the same phase of life. By an overwhelming nine-to-one ratio, boomers said their lives were more meaningful.

Fewer than half of boomers say that achieving the American Dream means "being wealthy," or "having power and influence," according to a survey conducted by RoperASW. While our parents defined the American Dream from the outside in, boomers tend to define it from the inside out.

In order of importance the four most essential aspects of life to midlife boomers are: spending time with family (61 percent), having a fulfilling relationship with a spouse or significant other (59 percent), staying healthy and fit (50 percent), and feeling good about ourselves (46 percent).

> **Sandy Smith:** *"My parents lived in another state when my kids were growing up. I was bound and determined that was not going to be the case with me. Every minute I get to spend with my grandson is precious."*

Whether or not we become effective grandparents will depend largely upon how we deal with the social, economic, and personal issues that affect us as we age.

"Boomers are going to have to learn how to be balanced in this phase of their lives," says Dr. Kornhaber. "They will still be quite active with their jobs and leisure time. Yet they will have a very broad range of family roles to play—mother, father, daughter, son, sister, brother, grandmother, and grandfather. They need to figure out how to balance these priorities.

"We are given extra years of life. I am in my seventies and I run every morning. When my grandfather was my age he was totally burned out. Aging is a bewildering kind of thing. The next generation is going to go through this same kind of bewilderment. At the same time it's exciting. Rather than take another job for money, I hope we get back to making sure we can help our children and grandchildren. This is especially true of boomer men who were not there as fathers."

> **Bob (Boppy) Giovanni:** *"I thought it was rewarding to be a father but being a grandpa is a gas!"*

Boomers have delayed every life stage transition, such as getting married and having children, so there's little reason to doubt that we will delay our retirement too. In fact, an AARP survey revealed that 80 percent of boomers plan to continue working long after age sixty-six or sixty-seven, when full Social Security benefits kick in for our generation. Among the reasons to keep working: Many of us haven't saved enough for this milestone, we like our high-paying professional careers, and we intend to continue working full- or part-time for the money, insurance, and/or the psychic benefits.

A 2003 report by the Public Policy Institute said that one third of working boomers do not have retirement coverage—not a traditional pension, nor a 401(k) account, nor an individual retirement account. As a result, many of us will work into our seventies out of necessity.

Delayed retirement could mean less time with the grandkids.

"There's no denying that people are retiring at a much later date," says prominent educator Barbara Bowman. "The availability of grand-parents as a support system has, in many cases, decreased because they are engaged actively in the workforce. Although the emotional support that grandparents are supposed to give their children and grandchil-dren may continue, very often it doesn't consist of their presence."

However, flex time at the office and telecommuting at home are offering many boomer nanas and papas more opportunities to spend needed time with their grandkids. But because Americans are living longer, many boomers also worry about the well-being of their retired parents and the possibility of big hospital and nursing-care bills.

"The boomers are the first generation in large numbers to become grandparents while their parents are still alive," says Dr. Martin. "You'll have multiple caregiving roles. You are involved in your chil-dren's and grandchildren's lives as well as your parents'. Who is going to provide for your elderly parents' needs and help out your adult chil-dren? When are you going to visit your parents? When are you going to see your grandchildren? These are issues which you must confront."

The shifting relationship between aging parents and their grown chil-dren can be fraught with emotional challenges. Among them: elderly parents who are becoming aware of their own vulnerability, the fear of mortality, the decline of people who used to be in charge of the extended family, and adult children still carrying grudges against their parents and siblings. Then there are those necessary delicate and troubling conversations about if or when to take over the elderly parents' finances, to move them out of the house and into assisted living, to take away the keys to the car, to arrange how they want to die.

"Baby boomers are used to achievement, trying new things and new experiences, and saying, 'I'm going to be the best damn caregiver out there,'" says Richard O'Boyle, of Eldercare. "Then they bump into the reality that this is a lot harder than they thought."

Disco diva Donna Summer, quoted on her role as a grand-mother of two: *"It's an honor. I'm just happy that I'm alive to see this great happening."*

Also thrown into the mix of today's new grandparent is the increasing number of grandchildren who live in nontraditional families and face bigotry and prejudice for having gay or interracial parents.

Not only that, more grandchildren are being raised by grandparents than ever before—a trend, experts say, that will steadily increase for boomers. A Census Bureau report cites drug abuse among parents, teen pregnancy, divorce, the rise of single-parent households, mental and physical illness, AIDS, child abuse, and imprisonment as the leading causes for the increase in both multigenerational households and households in which the grandparents act as primary caregivers. During the latest Iraqi war and occupation, grandparents plunged into parenthood again by taking care of the children of reservists and guardsmen who were called up for duty.

Vern Bengtson, professor of gerontology and sociology at the University of Southern California, also attributes the growth of grandparents raising kids to new laws on child endangerment, which have removed children from abusive-parent homes. He says there are pluses to these households. "Multigenerational families are becoming more important for social support," he says.

However, the reassembling of families through divorce, remarriage, and cohabitation begs the question: Will the divorced and remarried boomer grandparents maintain as healthy a relationship with their adult children, grandchildren, stepchildren, and stepgrandchildren as those grandparents whose families have remained intact? Mounting research shows that divorce and blended families threaten to weaken ties between generations.

> **Jane (Nona) Haglund:** *"I'm thrilled and proud to be a grandma. My heart just isn't big enough. I just love my grandson more than I ever dreamed I could."*

Dr. Martin believes aging boomers will not want to live out their lives in a multigenerational household. "People don't want to live that way unless it's a crisis or emergency. I hope we don't have to make that choice. What we want is 'intimacy at a distance.' We want to be close to our kids and grandkids but we don't want to live under one roof. We want our own life to be under our control." Regardless, he believes that boomers will find a way to handle these difficult situations.

No matter what kind of family the grandkids live in, we grandparents will be spending more money than ever before on them for necessities, from school supplies to clothes to medical bills to tuition. "Boomer grandparents will be sharing whatever they have for the sake of the grandchildren," says Dr. Martin.

Those who are healthy and enjoy an active lifestyle will influence their grandchildren, he adds. "You may have a more active grandparenting style and not be someone who visits only on birthdays and holidays. I envision a grandparent who takes the grandchildren on travels and exposes them to new experiences. Much depends on how economically secure boomers will be. The verdict is still out."

The size of the transfer of wealth from elderly parents to their boomer children might not be as large as once thought because Americans are living longer, to an all-time high of over seventy-seven years. Boomers' parents, saddled with soaring costs in health care and long-term care, are draining their nest eggs to fund their own extended retirements.

> **Dr. Anya (Baba) Luchow Liberman:** *"I melt as a grandmother. Nothing brings a bigger smile to my face than hearing the little ones on the phone saying 'Hi Baba.' I can't describe the feel-*

*ing in my gut when I see these children. I'm a touchy, feely mush.
I was that way with my children, but I didn't realize I could feel
this way even more."*

According to an AARP survey, 75 percent of boomers admit
they're more self-indulgent than their parents. Yet boomers understand that their lifestyle comes at a price—84 percent recognize that
they have to make more money and continue to work after retirement
age in order to retire. Twenty-three percent say they are counting on
an inheritance to help them. With this patchwork safety net, 65 percent of boomers feel confident that they will have enough to retire in
comfort. John Gist, associate director of the AARP Public Policy
Institute, says that while many boomers are better off than their parents were at the same age, "their expectations are also greater, and
some will find their resources falling short." By his estimate, only a
quarter of us will be comfortably set in retirement; at the other
extreme, a quarter will end their years in poverty with the rest falling
somewhere in between. As of 2001, only about 17 percent of boomers
had received any inheritance. The median inheritance was $47,909.

Regardless, boomer grandparents will spend an increasing amount
on gifts for their grandchildren, which in 2003 averaged $500 per
grandchild for grandparents of all ages. It all adds up to a $35 billion
industry that only keeps growing. With characteristic zeal and self-
absorption, we boomer grandparents are snapping up experiential
products that we can share and use with the youngsters. We don't
want to merely give them some nondescript toy; we want to enjoy the
gift too. That's why we are purchasing interactive computer games
that teach learning skills, nontraditional gifts such as wild animal
adoptions through wildlife organizations, games we can play with our
grandchildren, and toys and craft sets to assemble together. And, oh
yes, lots of grandkids' clothes. Some stores say grandparents now
account for more than a third of all its kiddie-gear sales, a 20 percent
jump in five years.

Chalk it up to supply and demand. While there are an estimated 70
million grandparents in the United States, the number of children per

family is near a thirty-year low. That's good news and bad news. On the upside, with fewer grandkids, grandparents can dote on them more. On the downside, there aren't enough grandkids to go around—and because of divorces, second marriages, and longer lives, grandparents and stepgrandparents are competing for face time.

For those boomers lucky enough to inherit money, they will spend it on acquiring personal experiences, whether it's traveling to an exotic locale, taking gourmet cooking lessons, or learning to play a musical instrument. And they will use the opportunity to introduce their passions to their grandchildren. They will want to give grandkids a wider range of experiences, particularly of things that boomers wish they could have experienced as kids but that their parents couldn't afford, such as space camp or computer camp and private lessons in painting, music, or other artistic endeavors.

"Those boomers with the resources will do the fun things with their grandchildren that they didn't do with their own kids because they didn't spend enough time or money," says Dr. Martin. "Boomers could get very close to their grandchildren. I can see the day when grandkids do things with their grandparents that they won't do with their own parents."

Marketing experts expect boomer grandparents to shell out big bucks to vacation with their grandkids, particularly on trips that can broaden the youngsters' minds. (After all, we're the generation that made *Europe on 5 Dollars a Day* a bestseller.) Eco-friendly cruise packages, river rafting, and other adventure tours will be major attractions. Grandparents who don't live near their grandchildren will spend freely on airplane and train tickets and road trips to visit them more frequently than older grandparents.

Summer Kircher, fifty-five-year-old grandmother of four, who took one grandchild to Italy on vacation: *"I'm not a baby-sitter. I like to do things with them. I envision our activities as becoming even more experiential as they get older."*

We certainly intend to keep up with the grandkids and not let our age slow us down. Mediamark Research, Inc., reports that the number of grandparents (those with grandkids under age eighteen) who play basketball and video games and hike increased, respectively, 227 percent, 208 percent, and 156 percent between 1988 and 2001. Meanwhile, the number of grandparents who collect stamps and play cards has risen at a much slower rate during that same period.

Boomer grandparents definitely will complain about not having enough time for all the things they want to do. "You'll hear that in the beginning of the grandparenting process," says Dr. Martin. "But grandparenting, like parenting, is a long-term progression. That scenario is more likely to happen when the grandchild is very young, under three years old. At that point, you are more helpful to the parent, fulfilling an active grandparenting role such as baby-sitting and helping out. It doesn't take as much involvement or energy.

"But once the grandchildren are five or older, that is a more crucial time to get involved because that's when the kids have an awareness of the grandparent. That's also the time when the boomers start thinking of phasing out their active work life. In your late forties and fifties you're still in the midlife phase. The question to ask yourself is: 'How much can I accomplish in the remaining time I have left in my work life?' Boomers are still going full speed ahead in their work. But that soon will change. As they get into their mid-fifties and as their grandchildren get older, boomers will find opportunities to be involved with them."

Because the average American family is smaller than past generations, boomer grandparents have a greater opportunity to be involved in the individual growth and development of their grandkids, Dr. Martin adds. "The bonds between grandchildren and their boomer grandparents will become much stronger if merely by the fact that boomers don't tend to have a lot of children. With fewer grandkids, the boomers will be much closer to those they do have. Fewer relationships mean each one can be more special. Boomers will invest more time and energy into their grandchildren."

And we'll invest in our grandchildren's education by helping to pay for lessons and tuitions in schools of the family's choice and by salting money away for the grandkids' college expenses.

Linda (Mimi) Gray: *"I have a busy life with many interests, but for sheer joy and pleasure, none compare to being with my granddaughter."*

Compared to previous generations, boomer grandparents will be more intellectually curious, active, worldly, and driven by principles and doing what's right, according to the marketing firm SRI. "The primary difference with the new wave of grandparents is they'll have a lot more resources— not just education and money, but also self-confidence, intellectualism, and global awareness," says SRI senior consultant Kathy Whitehouse.

Another big change in the grandparenting landscape is the first generation of boomer grandmothers who have their own careers. They are more likely to be college-educated, to be employed outside the home, divorced or remarried, and to have a sense of themselves as independent people, according to Jean Giles-Sims, a sociologist at Texas Christian University. Even grandmothers who don't work are different from previous generations, according to Giles-Sims. They're more active in their community, they travel, and they volunteer.

However, not all boomer grandparents fit this profile. Despite the increasingly larger shift toward more engaged grandparenting, Giles-Sims has uncovered a simultaneous smaller trend toward more remote grandparenting—those who are cut off from their grandchildren either by distance or conflict with the adult children. In addition, many new grandparents will continue to perpetuate the image and thinking of the traditional grandparent but perhaps with a younger-looking face.

Boomers are nothing if not contradictory and a little self-absorbed. We might remain liberal in spirit, but we're slowly, steadily, inexorably growing more conservative in our politics and lifestyles. But that doesn't mean we'll be stuffy old codgers. Quite the contrary; it's just that we will be vocal in trying to make life better for our grandkids. In fact, say the experts, boomers will, if we haven't already, embrace many of the same values that we had trashed in our youth.

Let's be honest. The boomer-led social revolution of the '60s really did a number on anyone over thirty—especially grandparents. It characterized our elders as outmoded human Edsels. No longer did wisdom equate with experience. "It's what's happening now." . . . "If it feels good do it." . . . "Do your own thing." Huge numbers of boomers rejected the traditional values and principles that had been the guiding force for our grandparents and parents.

It took us a while, but we're rediscovering those ideals. And, yes, many of us do feel a little guilty for having belittled and disowned the beliefs of the very people who gave us the self-assurance and security to be our free-to-be selves. Now we're turning that guilt into action.

Observed historians William Strauss and Neil Howe, "A growing chorus of social critics is noticing a Boom-led 'New Puritanism' in circa-1990 America. Fortyish Americans are beginning to police 'politically correct' behavior, pass 'anti-ugly' zoning ordinances, punish students for 'inappropriately directed laughter,' circulate 'Green Lifestyle' guides and attach 'Green Seals' to products, ban obscene music, promote 'chastity,' and even support novel forms of corporal punishment and boot-camp incarceration that [their parents] would never have imagined—and that Boomers, two decades ago, would have considered fascist."

Members of the Me Generation "have seen the evil of their ways," says Dr. Buffington. "Liberalism to conservatism has a forty-year swing and that pendulum is definitely swinging away from liberalism. I think we are going back because we feel our culture is so out of control. We are responsible for it, so what is happening now is overcorrection.

"You always return to the familiar. Always. In a crisis situation— and many people believe our society is in a moral crisis—you tend to believe that whatever worked once for you will work again. The kinds of behavior we learned during the Beaver Cleaver era are the same ones boomers want to see for our grandchildren. I wouldn't be surprised if boomers return to the Ozzie and Harriet look again."

Boomers will seek to unite the generations, much like it was before the social revolution, says Dr. Brazelton. We're finally becoming aware of the longing that we missed when we failed to involve our parents in the lives of our kids, he said. "I think the concept of the extended family was lost in your generation probably because of the generation gap. That was really tragic because that left your generation with nobody to fall back on when you got into trouble. And raising children can be full of trouble. This longing [to involve elders in family life] will push boomers to be better grandparents."

> **Alisa (Nana) Dollar:** *"Grandchildren are bright-eyed, innocent little blessings. It's amazing to see in your own children the extension of your spouse and yourself—and to see it extended yet further through your grandchildren is truly a remarkable happening."*

Grandchildren present boomers with a Mulligan, another shot at being there for the family. "Even though boomers are active and egocentric, we will come to the awareness that maybe we should have invested more in our own children," says Dr. Martin. "But it's too late to do that for them, so maybe we'll have a second chance to do that with our grandchildren."

Dr. Buffington agrees. "Boomers raised hell in the sixties, their kids in the seventies, their blood pressure in the eighties, and their personal deficits in the nineties. Now as grandparents, it's time for redemption. They will get involved with their grandchildren if for no other reason than to undo what they screwed up in their own kids. They get another chance to show their paternal and maternal mettle, not to mention assuaging their guilt. They should make better teachers of morality. Having been there and done that, they'll keep their grandkids from going to those same places and doing those same things.

"Boomers are now dealing with the concept of immortality and that as parents we were lousy. We see it, to some degree, in how our children turned out and that bothers us. Through grandparenthood, we are now convinced that we have a reprieve, a dispensation from God. We have another chance to help rear children. We see grandparenting as a way to absolve ourselves of guilt from being so job-conscious, so corporate-conscious that the family came second. We may have failed our families in the seventies and eighties, but, by God, we're not going to fail again."

Dr. Martin doesn't think we should beat ourselves up over any per-ceived parenting faults. "We have done a better job of raising children than people think. Yes, we've had to juggle jobs and family. But we engaged our children in all kinds of activities—soccer, music lessons, and so many other things that we, as children, didn't have the oppor-tunity to do. We'll no doubt want to encourage our grandchildren to be involved in all sorts of activities."

And this could lead to another issue. We're likely to be quite vocal in how our grandchildren are raised, says Dr. Martin, adding that the activist side of us "could translate into overly active grandparents, more than perhaps their adult children would like."

We boomers have been raised to question, argue, and ultimately disobey orders that aren't in sync with our own beliefs. We may be just as assertive with our adult children when it comes to caring for our grandkids.

"When boomers were younger we didn't trust older people, but that won't stop boomer grandparents from wanting to serve in some sort of a consulting mode in the lives of their adult children," says Dr. Martin. "The current grandparenting mode is, 'Ask me, and I'll give you advice.' The boomer grandparents are likely to have the attitude, 'I'll give you advice; take it or leave it.' We won't wait to be asked for advice.

"The baby boom generation has changed the agenda of almost everything in this country—husbands, wives, families. I wouldn't be surprised to see boomer grandparents be a bit too bossy with their adult children [in how the grandchildren are raised] to the extent that the middle generation might get a little upset about it.

"The middle generation typically negotiates between the grandpar-ents and the grandchildren such things as the amount of contact and the quality of the interaction. That might change with the boomer grandparents. They may build their own bridge directly to their grand-children and disregard the middle generation."

If the experts are right, it's two thumbs up for the boomer grandpar-ents. "I think there is good news," says Dr. Kornhaber. "Today's new grandparents have really started to think about more emotional, spiritual, and family imperatives to life now that they've passed the boundaries of materialism and the Me generation. The pendulum is swinging back, and I am seeing a growing consciousness about the importance of the family."

Jane (Nona) Haglund: *"I talk to him [her two-year-old grandson Anson] all the time. [Her daughter] Kim gives him her cell phone just to get him out of her hair. When she's driving, she has me on speed dial, punches my number, and then gives Anson the phone. I love hearing 'Hi, Nona.' Sometimes his dad has Anson leave me messages on my answering machine. I haven't erased any of them."*

Things from Our Childhood That Our Grandkids Likely Will Never See

Blackjack and Beeman's gum

Powerhouse candy bars

licorice records

wax teeth, lips, and mustaches

wax Coke-shaped bottles with colored sugar water

candy lipstick

candy cigarettes

Fizzies

soda pop machines that dispense glass bottles

pull tabs that snap off soda cans

home milk delivery in glass bottles with cardboard stoppers

movies preceded by cartoons and newsreels

party lines

rotary phones

sock hops

winter rubber boots with metal latches

coonskin hats

P.F. Flyers

bouffant hairdos

spoolies

hair dryers with plastic caps

butch wax

tin-can telephones

peashooters

cork popguns

roll of cap-gun caps

Howdy Doody puppets

Beanie and Cecil dolls

two-bladed ice skates that clip onto shoes

roller skates that clip onto shoes

roller skate keys

S & H Green Stamps and Plaid Stamps

metal lunchboxes

Winky Dink kits for drawing on the TV screen

crystal radios

console hi-fis with 78s

45-rpm records

hand-crank wringers on tub washing machines

slide rules

levered metal ice trays

mimeograph paper

carbon paper

flashbulbs

eight-track tape decks

home movie cameras

Dick and Jane readers

Good Vibrations

The Expectant Grandparent

The Age Thing

ONE DAY YOU PICK UP THE PHONE and learn you're going to be a grandparent. You're ecstatic (assuming the call is not from your unmarried daughter who's dating a Marilyn Manson wannabe). You're thrilled. You're jubilant. And at the height of your joy, you reach a sobering conclusion: grand + parent = old.

More of us than might care to admit probably have encountered a negative feeling or two over becoming a grandparent. But that's natural, say the experts who add that we shouldn't get mired in guilt or self-recrimination if we experience such contrary emotions. They are most often caused by our fixation on youthfulness or by our inability to be psychologically ready for this role.

The happiness of becoming nanas and papas sometimes gives way to tinges of sadness or even depression because the news forces us to confront the fact that we're no longer as young as we think. Like Arte Johnson's decrepit geezer getting whacked over the head by Ruth Buzzi's little old lady, we're knocked senseless by the reality of aging.

So what if your heart rate is better than it was fifteen years ago or that you look and feel sexier than ever (especially after botox injections and liposuction)? Like it or not, you're motoring down the road of life with brakes that don't work. You've passed the territories of childhood and parenthood and are entering grandparenthood where the neon sign on the roadside diner flashes, "Last Stop Before Senility." Your years are numbered, and they total less than the sum of Beatles hits.

Wasn't it just yesterday you weren't trusting anybody over thirty? Now you don't trust anybody under that age.

Linda (Mimi) Gray: *"When I got the 'Mom, I'm pregnant'
call, the first thing I did after I hung up was rush into the bathroom and look at myself in the mirror, wondering, 'Do I look like
a grandmother?'"*

Afraid that grandparenting will make you feel old? Tough, say the
experts. Your grandkids are going to think you're old no matter what
your age—even if you are too young to remember *Hopalong Cassidy* on
Saturday morning TV. But it's okay because kids don't care. "Even
though Grandma is running around now in Spandex, the kids see her
as someone with age, and that's just fine with them," says Dr. Perry
Buffington. "Kids see grandparents as timeless."

So accept your fate. Grandparenting may not sound sexy in our
age-obsessed society, but it definitely has its own cachet.

Judy (Grammy) Ernest, in the *Cleveland Plain Dealer*:
*"When our [first] grandson was born, I kept trying to evade the
truth by giving myself a title other than 'Grandma.' I requested
'Foxy,' but my son and daughter-in-law nixed it. We settled on
'Grammy.' It has been an apt title. My two grandchildren make
me feel like an award-winner. And, they are keeping me young."*

If your ego is still swirling with mixed emotions over your impending status, you might need a little attitude adjustment. Grasp this: Your
child is gifting you with a wonderful new human being, part of your
living legacy. That's cause for celebration, for you to get psyched. A
precious little person is about to enter your life and capture your heart.
Joy to the world! If anything, you ought to feel the envy of those
friends who're wondering when they'll become grandparents too.

Peggie: *"I am forty-three years old and just found out I will be
a grandmother in seven months! I am really struggling with the
idea and certainly can't stand the idea of being called Grannie,
Grandma, or Nana . . . What am I to do? . . . I am sure I
will get used to the idea, but for now I am in shock and still feel
that I am too young to be known as 'Grannie.'"*

Only 39 percent of boomers between the ages of forty-five and fifty-four years old are completely satisfied with how they feel about themselves, according to a study conducted by trend-tracker RoperASW for AARP. Baby boomers feel that their youth is fading. When Americans hit forty-five, the majority say they stop looking young and that their peak attractiveness is now passed. Sixty-eight percent of those forty-five to fifty-four say that on a given day, they look "middle-aged." However, half say that they're not at all depressed by aging and nearly as many say they are very accepting of the changes that come with age.

If you're fretting over this age thing, put a new spin on your upcoming role. Assuming you're healthy and active and have cleverly hidden your gray hair (you men still have hair, don't you?), you probably don't look your age. So play up the fact that you are, or will be, a grandparent. Don't be shy. Announce it wherever you go—the fitness center, the union meeting, the chiropractor. It'll do you good.

> **Kathryn:** *"When I first became a grandmother, people would say, 'You don't look like a grandma.' I loved it. Slowly over the last seven years those comments have diminished. Do I miss it? Sure. But being a young-looking grandmother isn't as important to me as it once was. It's more important for me to be the best grandmother I can be."*

We need to boot out of our consciousness those lingering childhood perceptions of grandparents as being wrinkled senior citizens. Heck, your parents or grandparents were probably your age—or even younger—when they became nanas and papas. They just looked older to you because you were seeing them through the eyes of a child or young parent.

> **Sue (Nana) Crawford, fifty-two:** *"I don't see myself as an old lady, not like my grandparents. Hmmm. My grandmother was forty-five when I was born, and I always thought she was an old lady. Oh, well, I'm sure my grandkids [both under the age of two] will think the same thing about me because the bag boys at the grocery store think I'm old now."*

You probably look much younger and better than your mom and dad when you made them grandparents, right? They were set in their ways, watching TV in the BarcaLounger, going to Tupperware parties, and playing golf. They weren't like you (okay, except for the golf). They didn't skydive, run 10-K's, or in-line skate. Did people ever mistake your mom for your sister à la Grandma Naomi Judd and her daughter Wynonna? Could your father hop across the stage like Grandpa Mick Jagger singing "Let's Spend the Night Together"?

Pamela Faust, a fifty-six-year-old grandmother married to a man eighteen years her junior: *"Some days I feel nineteen, sometimes I feel like 109. Usually I'm somewhere in between. I am in total denial of my 'real' age. I admit it. I refuse to allow that number to rule my life. I color my hair to reflect the way I feel, because I don't feel old enough to have gray hair yet."*

We aging boomers are determined to redefine what it means to get older. As TV news personality Linda Ellerbee wrote about turning fifty, "We are a generation that believes we can have it our way, mainly because we so often have. Most of us do not face this age thing gracefully. We fight. Some harder than others. Some of us go into heavy denial. We can exercise ourselves to the skin and bone. We can eat nothing but broccoli. We can pay the plastic surgeon, dye our hair, date (and/or marry) much younger men and women . . . quit old careers . . . and change old habits, but we cannot stop time. We cannot go back and be who we were. Those people are gone."

Gone are the flower children, potheads, go-go dancers, grunts, grads, yippies, and yuppies that we once were. We're grandparents now. And, for some, it's unsettling.

Luisa Kroll, writing for *Forbes.com*: *"The boomers are in denial and they will remain there, refusing to step aside or to make concessions to the aging process. Why should they adjust to reality, when they have spent their lives forcing reality to adjust to them?"*

"I had a hard time at first acknowledging that I was going to be a grandmother," admits Dr. Susan Ginsberg. "It seemed like other people would think I was so old.

"It's not uncommon for you to experience some denial. Grandparenting is not part of your self-image. I know many people became grandparents reluctantly—kicking and screaming because it was an assault on their self-image. But most people get used to it very quickly. When you see friends your age becoming grandparents, then it makes you feel better. There's a whole world of grandparents who look and act young. They work and are busy doing things. But there's still so much focus in society on being young that it's stupid.

"When my granddaughter was seven she told me, 'You're not a real grandma.' 'Why not?' I asked. She said, 'You don't have gray hair, you work, and you go to exercise class. What's wrong with you?' I told her, 'There are lots of different kinds of grandmas and some feel and look younger than others.'"

Bob (Boppy) Giovanni: *"I was really happy with the news of being a grandfather. But, I confess, there was a part of me that said, 'Man, you're getting old!' "*

Our culture works against grandparenthood by focusing on looking forever young, laments grandparenting guru Dr. Arthur Kornhaber. "Grandparenting isn't sexy. According to society, if I'm a grandparent, I'm old. One guy I know wanted his grandsons to call him 'Uncle'; another didn't want to be known as 'Grandpa' because he wouldn't be able to flirt with the secretaries. Grandparenting consciousness is not recognized or savored in this country. Grandparenting as a function is equated with old age, and no one wants to be old.

"Boomer grandparents need to embrace this next phase of their life. We have to change our culture so 'old' means you're ennobled, you're powerful, you're important. But our value system is so corrupt, ridiculous, and unrealistic that those traits of aging don't fit."

You must retool your thinking and get pumped up about this new stage of your life and enjoy it, he adds. "As you age, you have an enormous opportunity to grow, to become more forgiving, less judgmental, more accepting, and more compassionate. You should talk openly about the importance of elders doing what we've been hardwired to do for all of human existence—nurture and teach the younger generation while the middle generation is working. The consciousness of the importance of the family connection between young and old needs to be raised to a new level.

"The boomer generation is starting to understand this and develop a new image of aging in our culture. Hopefully society will be receptive to this idea because the power of aging can be a pretty sexy idea once you get rid of the notion that old age means playing shuffleboard and watching yourself go down the tubes. Our culture must appreciate the usefulness of elders. Selling that concept is a big challenge for the boomer grandparents."

> **Kathryn:** *"At fifty-four, I was thinking I looked pretty good for my age. But I got a reality check during a trip to the beach when our five-year-old grandson Danny piped up from the backseat, 'Nana, are you gonna die?' Perplexed by the question, I said, 'No, why did you ask me that?' Danny replied, 'Because you're old, and old people die.'"*

Even if you're hung up on age, your grandchildren won't be. "Children don't have age prejudice," says Dr. Kornhaber. "They don't see a fifty-year-old person. They see a grandparent who they think is wonderful and who they love deeply. Children will tell me what about their grandparent makes them happy, what makes him or her worth something to them, why they adore their grandparent. It has nothing to do with anything physical like how young the grandparent looks. Besides, wrinkles are interesting to kids anyway.

"It's this idea of 'I am how I look and not how people feel about me' that gets boomers into trouble. When you age, there's nothing you can do about things sagging and joints creaking. That's normal. You are going to have to deal with how you view self-worth. It's very important to minimize this kind of physical attraction as a basis for self-esteem. There must be a shift in values."

Are You Ready?

As an expectant or new grandparent, you might have come to grips with the age issue, yet still might not be ready psychologically, Dr. Kornhaber says. "Readiness for grandparenthood depends on attaining an optimum developmental state and having the time, the appropriate psychological and philosophical attitudes, and the appropriate family situation to be a grandparent.

"After raising their children, everyone needs a rest to recenter themselves and their identity. Hopefully they are afforded an opportunity to fulfill some of their own private needs and dreams. Eventually that drive to become a grandparent bubbles up and you're ready to nurture grandchildren. That's the ideal situation."

Some people in Dr. Kornhaber's Grandparent Study said they wanted to wait until they were older before becoming grandparents. Other unready grandparents hoped to pursue their personal goals full-time or had preconceived ideas about the right time in their lives to be grandparents. One woman told him, "I'll be happy to be a grandmother when I'm sixty-five, not now when I'm only fifty-two. I've got some time for myself for the first time in my life. This is 'me' time." A few people in the study were not thrilled about becoming grandparents because they felt too overburdened with other caregiving responsibilities.

Bliss, reminds Dr. Kornhaber, is dependent on the emotional happiness of the entire family and those closest to us. "We used to define ourselves by our relationships to our friends and family." Maybe that's what we should bring back into vogue, he says.

> **Anne Bernays, writing in *Town & Country Monthly*:** "I tried hard to be cool about the looming first grandchild . . . but my unconscious tricked me into misreading the nameplate on a Pontiac as 'Grand Ma' when it was clearly 'Grand Am.'"

When we learn that we're going to be grandparents, it's common for us to take stock of ourselves and count all the successes, failures, and unfulfilled dreams. You're in your late forties or early fifties and the truth is you're not ever going to throw passes for the Miami Dolphins or head an internationally-acclaimed fashion house or cut a record with Jimmy Buffett. You made choices. Now, as you reach the grandparenting stage, you're ready to make more choices. Take this opportunity to rethink your priorities for the remaining years of your life. What is it that's really worth doing? Grandparenting should rank high on the list.

Meanwhile, don't fuss over the strange emotions you might experience over news of your impending new role as a grandparent.

"If you have mixed feelings about becoming a grandparent, relax. They prove you're only being human," says Dr. Buffington. "You don't need to feel ashamed over that angst or anguish. Accept them and even talk about them. Most people usually work through these feelings pretty quickly. The moment you hold that grandchild and bond with that baby, those conflicting feelings should melt away."

Here's what cyber-columnist Pat Connolly wrote (quoted here in edited form, with her permission) when she learned that she was going to be a nana at the age of forty-six:

"Hi! My name is Pat and I'm a grandmother."

I was sure that this is how I would introduce myself from now on, like a confession at an AA meeting. Or worse yet, I wouldn't have to say anything—everyone would just know by looking.

It was very traumatic the night I found out my daughter was pregnant. As I sat looking at her and her proud husband toasting with a bottle of champagne, all I could see in my mind was a bent, white-haired, wrinkled woman whose total life became dedicated to a small child. Grandmother!

As the weeks turned into months, I noticed whenever the fact came up that I was going to be a grandmother, I had a sense of wonder followed by an upset feeling. How could I let anyone know what was going on inside my head? Everyone thought it was such a good idea. I must be thrilled.

I began to think I wasn't such a great person. I mean, people were saying grandmothers-to-be are coming into a great part of their lives. (I noticed the ones saying this were mostly the white-haired grandmothers.) How come it didn't look that way to me? What's wrong here?

I tried to put myself at ease as I peered intensely into my mirror. "Well, I'll be a very young-looking grandmother and I won't fall all over the kid. I'll enjoy my time with him or her and then go on with my life."

As my daughter grew bigger, I became more concerned about my feelings. I wouldn't volunteer anything about the impending arrival to my friends. When someone asked me a direct question about the pregnancy, I acted like everything was really great with me. I was supposed to be excited and glad, right? I felt like a traitor. I asked myself, "What's wrong with me? Why am I not excited? Does anyone else feel this way?" I couldn't talk to anyone. Who ever heard of a grandmother-to-be who wasn't really excited and who hated the whole idea?

I jotted down every negative thought I had about becoming a grandmother. Then I tried to recall its origin. You know the one about the white-haired grandmothers? That came from meeting my grandmother's friends at her club when I was eight years old. Even bleached blondes looked like white-haired ladies. It was so funny—and revealing—to discover the origin of each thought, especially the one "Grandmothers are not sexy." When my oldest daughter was born, my aunt called my dad and said, "Sam, do you know what this makes you?" He replied, "Old—and sleeping with a grandmother!"

That stuck with me. When I became an expectant grand-mother, I unthinkingly wore old nightgowns and lower-heeled shoes and didn't wear bright-colored clothes or things that appeared too young for me. I began behaving in what I consid-ered to be a more appropriate way for a grandmother. Yuck!

But then I decided to replace those negative thoughts with positive ones like, "Grandmothers have a lot more time to be athletic." "Grandmothers take care of their bodies so they can stay sexy." "Grandmothers have a lot more freedom to do and be what they want."

I began to practice, practice, practice creating new thoughts. The more advanced the pregnancy became, the more adept I became at changing my old way of thinking. As time drew closer

to the baby's arrival, I was very happy about becoming a grandmother and looking for ways to make this time fun and exciting.

Party Time

As Three Dog Night so eloquently put it, "Celebrate! Celebrate!
Dance to the music!"

Make a big deal out of your impending grandparenthood. Why
should the new or expectant parents get all the glory and attention?
Host your own party as a festive way to tell your friends about your new
role. For that matter, the next time your friends announce they are going
to be, or have just become, grandparents, throw a bash for them.

> **Michelle (Grammy) Davies:** *"Our friends are always looking
> for excuses to have parties, so when we announced we were going
> to be grandparents, they threw a party for us. Everyone came as a
> fictional grandparent—you know, like Heidi's grandpa and
> Grandmama Addams. It was wild."* (How much do you want
> to bet that everyone came with canes and gray-haired wigs?)

We have wedding showers and baby showers, so why not grandparent
showers? Be a trendsetter and host one for the new or expectant grandparents. Don't necessarily restrict the shower to women. Couples are
often invited to other kinds of showers, so this should be no exception.

Forget the gag gifts and go for something practical. After all, how
many new or soon-to-be nanas and papas have everything they need
for those times when the baby comes for a visit? A trip to the local
baby store can overwhelm rookie grandparents with items that they
didn't know they needed—and probably didn't even know were on the
market.

Some suggested inexpensive items for a shower:

- toys to start a grandparent's collection
- picture frame or album
- safety kit that includes electrical outlet covers and safety
  latches

- books for the grandchild
- how-to books for the grandparent (like this one!)
- baby shampoo, soap, towels, and washcloths
- child's eating utensils and unbreakable plates and cups
- safety gate
- baby blanket
- baby monitor

For big-ticket items that two or more persons could purchase together, consider:

- crib
- high chair
- car seat
- umbrella stroller

Peggy (Granma) Minacci: *"When I was an expectant grandmother, a friend brought over some toys. I said David and Melissa [the parents-to-be] would really appreciate them. She said, 'They're not for the parents. They're for you when your grandchild comes to visit.' It hadn't occurred to me that I'd need things like that at my house."*

Rite of Passage

Besides showers and parties, mark this moment in a more special, poignant way—a personal gesture or ceremony that adds some significance to your upcoming grandparenthood.

Here's where you take the time and effort to reflect on your new role—how you want to fit into your grandchild's life, what she means to you, what you hope to mean to her. This rite of passage is a way to commemorate your love and involvement in the family. It also helps make grandparenting more than an abstract concept and gives you the opportunity to appreciate your life and your loved ones.

You can create a rite in whatever way suits you—a quiet dinner with your mate at a special restaurant to talk about your feelings; a poem, letter, or song written to the newborn child; a visit to the family gravesite to contemplate the link between the past and future; the handcrafting of an item (such as a piece of pottery, sculpture, or wood-carving) that symbolizes this new status. Whatever you choose to do, the rite will heighten your awareness of becoming a grandparent.

Jane (Nana) Trebble: *"We planted a peach tree to honor our grandson Jeremy. As the tree grows, so too will Jeremy. I can't wait until we can all eat peaches from his tree. We plan to grow a tree for each of our other grandchildren—assuming we'll have more."*

Jane (Nona) Haglund: *"To mark Anson's birth, we planted a lemon tree in the backyard. I also started a journal and write things about him. When I'm in the nursing home years from now, I hope I will remember to give it to him."*

Tom (Grandpa) Andersen: *"My wife and I sat down and we each wrote a letter to our granddaughter Sara shortly after she was born. We told her how much we loved her and what kind of grandparents we promised to be. We sealed our letters and put them in her hope chest. The letters really forced us to contemplate on what it means to be a grandparent. It'll be cool to see what she thinks when she reads our letters."*

Time to Cram

If you haven't already, now is a good time for you to brush up on the latest in prenatal care, birthing, postnatal care, and child development. You'll save yourself plenty of aggravation by being on the same page as the expectant parents. By not hitting the books, you risk acting as annoyingly out-of-touch as your elders were when you started a family.

"Read the books that the parents-to-be are reading so you can speak the same language," suggests Dr. T. Berry Brazelton. "It's important for you to keep up with the changes that are going on in parenting."

We had *Dr. Spock's Baby and Child Care* as our authority when we were young parents. Today's moms and dads are parenting bookworms who have access to thousands of books on the subject, not to mention magazines, videos, audiotapes, CDs, DVDs, and Web sites.

"Young parents are ODing on information," says Dr. Buffington. "They want to learn everything they can so they can do an incredibly good job of parenting. Unfortunately, they think that the knowledge needs to come from outside of them when the truth is that good, old-fashioned common sense will serve them, and their children, well."

Nevertheless, you need to know what's in their heads so you'll at least have some understanding about their decisions (not that there's much you can do if you disagree with them—but more about that in a later chapter). Boy, are there decisions for them to make: Will your grandchild make his big entrance in a hospital, birthing center, or at home? In a tub, a bed, or delivery room? With an obstetrician or a certified nurse midwife? Will the mother manage pain with analgesic drugs (morphine is out), patient-controlled analgesia, epidural anesthesia, self-hypnosis, or bite-the-bullet willpower? Will the baby be breast-fed or bottle-fed? Will the parents have your grandson circumcised? Will they bank the baby's cord-blood? Will they practice co-sleeping? By reading what the parents-to-be are reading, you'll get a degree of comfort in learning the rationale behind their choices. And, who knows, you might learn something.

Today's parents have a slate of products with brand names that might seem new to you, like Boppy, Snugli, and Nuk. Digital thermometers are placed in babies' ears, under armpits, or on foreheads. Teddy bears play soothing womb sounds while voice-activated cribs begin rocking at babies' first cries.

Have you heard about Bradley, LeBoyer, Odent, and Gamper? No, it's not a cover band for Crosby, Stills, Nash, and Young. Actually, they're names of popular childbirth methods. If you'd like to know more about what goes on in childbirth classes, ask your son or daughter if you can sit in on a session or two. Most instructors will welcome grandparents. Many hospitals and birthing centers offer special classes for grandparents-to-be, as do some pediatricians' or obstetricians' offices, so call around for classes nearest you.

Some simple tips from the experts:

- Be informed. From the start of your daughter's or daughter-in-law's pregnancy, keep pace with the expectant parents by using a pregnancy guide to track the stages of the fetus's development.
- Be attentive. Listen with enthusiasm and a positive attitude to the couple's pregnancy updates. Show a lot of patience and understanding during those stressful moments that pop up over the nine-month period.
- Be supportive, even if you don't agree with the birthing plans the couple make. Remember, it's their birth and their baby.
- Be available to help the couple with chores or errands, especially during the last trimester. Let them know you are available, but wait for them to ask you.
- Be ready. Collect baby equipment for when the infant visits your home.

Oh, yeah, there's one more important thing you should do before the baby arrives. Sit down with the parents-to-be, and in an honest heart-to-heart, discuss the role you're going to play as a grandparent.

I've Got to Be Me

Defining Your Grandparenting Role

The Big Gig

WHAT KIND OF NANA OR PAPA WILL YOU BE? The formal elder who shows interest and concern in the grandkids but adopts a hands-off policy? The informal fun-seeker who enjoys getting down and dirty with the grandkids? The surrogate who cares for the grandkids while the parents are working or absent? The distant figure who emerges from the shadows on birthdays, holidays, and special occasions?

Give it some serious thought, because you're going to be a grandparent for the rest of your life. In fact, you'll likely be one for more than half your adult life, not only because you're still relatively young but because you should live much longer than previous grandparents did.

This is no lame honorary position granted you simply because you have a child who's had a child. Your role is much more crucial and vital to the family than you think. Don't take our word for it. Listen to what the experts have to say:

- Dr. T. Berry Brazelton: "I think grandparents are more important than they ever were. With both parents working and the divorce rate rising, it's really critical for the grandparents to be there as a steady beacon for their grandchildren."

- Dr. Perry Buffington: "How important is being a grandparent today? More than you can possibly imagine! I say that with an exclamation point."

- Dr. Arthur Kornhaber: "I'm saying you count and you can change things for the better. Grandparents are terribly, terribly important to their families, especially to their grandchildren."

Research supports their views. The grandparent-grandchild bond is second in emotional importance only to that of the parent-child bond, according to the Grandparent Study. In confirming that grandparents and grandchildren deeply affect each other's lives, the study found that children who enjoy close relationships with at least one grandparent:

- feel accepted "as is" and even "adored"
- are more emotionally secure than those who have no such ties
- gain comfort in knowing they have a place to go—an "emotional sanctuary"—in times of trouble
- extend their love for their grandparents to all older people, have a positive image of aging, and are less likely to be ageist
- show greater respect for parents in households that foster the grandparent-grandchild relationship
- have an enriched understanding of the world because of what their grandparents teach them about earlier times and ways of living
- feel rooted in the past and enjoy a sense of belonging to a "family ego"

According to Native American beliefs, when you are grandparenting, you are nurturing not just your own grandchildren but seven generations yet unborn. You are making a difference in the lives of your grandkids and enjoying their personalities, and at the same time the rewards of your grandparenting extend well into the future.

Most new grandparents today have little idea what a lasting, positive impact they can make in the lives of their grandchildren. What will your grandkids say about you fifteen or twenty years from now? Perhaps they will echo the responses of college students who took part in a study by Dr. Gregory Sanders and Debra Trygstad of North Dakota State University.

The researchers found that 81 percent of the students described their relationship with the grandparent they saw most often as "extremely important." The majority said their grandparent kept them informed of family heritage (83.6 percent), gave them money (69.6 percent), provided emotional support (66.7 percent), and offered personal advice (63.4 percent). Their love for their grandparent didn't diminish as both grew older. Although 71.5 percent of the students saw their grandparent no more than monthly, 81 percent said this amount of contact was less than they desired.

"The love between a grandparent and grandchild is unconditional," says Dr. Kornhaber. "It's the simplest and least complicated intense human love bond. It's, 'I love you because you exist.' Jean-Paul Sartre said he could make his grandmother go into raptures of joy just by being hungry. This unconditional love is incredibly empowering for children.

"If grandparents did not exist, children surely would invent them. Children feel a natural connection between themselves and their grandparents. They exhibit a strong emotional need for close attachment to at least one grandparent. When they see each other, they get very happy and light up."

You've been freed from all the duties and constraints of a parent, so you can now savor the role of a grandparent. Dr. Brazelton is fond of saying, "Grandparents show children the mountaintops, while parents must teach them the drudgeries of how to get there."

Creating Your Role

While you await the birth of your grandchild, try to figure out what your individual grandparenting role is. What part do you want to play? Keep in mind that your part is not scripted for you, so you get to make up your own role—one that fits your particular active, working lifestyle yet still addresses your grandparenting goals.

To help you get started, ask yourself the following questions:

- How much time can I give my grandchild?
- How involved do I want to be in his life as an infant, a toddler, a preschooler?
- How much does his family need me to handle such chores as baby-sitting or running errands?
- How much am I willing to alter my life at home and work to be with my grandchild?
- What kind of relationship do I want to have with him?
- How can I become someone special in his life?

- What are my needs?
- What image do I want to portray?
- How do I want to be remembered?

There are no right or wrong answers. Every nana and papa is different, every situation unique. For a little inspiration, look at the traits that you admired in other grandparents. Just remember that you can't shape your role adequately if you feel obligated to match an unrealistic image of your grandparents, thereby feeling guilty if you fail. Figure out what qualities they had that you want to emulate. But create your own identity.

Kathryn: *"After I received the news from our daughter Allison that I was going to be a grandmother, my reaction of 'Wow, this is great!' turned into, 'Oh my God. Now what do I do? What kind of a grandmother do I want to be? Can I, should I, be like Grandma Lang?'*

"My grandmother was wonderful. She was a large woman who lived on a farm and could do just about everything. She patiently taught me to cook, knit, quilt, sew, and garden.

"After Allison's call I wondered, 'Am I going to have to do all those things for my grandchildren? I don't like baking cookies. Sewing? Knitting? It's cheaper to buy clothes. And I never was very good at those things anyway.'

"But then I realized a grandmother's love and attraction to her grandchild is as natural and deep as the love she felt toward her own babies. Some ways of showing that love will always remain the same. But as times change, so do grandparenting styles.

"So I don't bake cookies. I love to travel. What fun it will be to take the grandchildren to the Florida Keys, Manhattan, and Disney World. We'll introduce them to our interests, like archaeology, photography, and hiking. We'll outfit them with backpacks and hike along the Appalachian Trail, climb rocks on the Blue Ridge Mountains, and raft down the Nantahala.

"But maybe I'll make cookies after all. For some reason, cookies and grandmothers still seem to go together."

"The basic role of the grandparent hasn't changed at all—it's the unqualified love and support of your adult children and your grandchildren," says noted educator Barbara Bowman, president of the Erikson Institute. "And that doesn't change no matter what other stresses and strains there are in life."

If you want to be the most effective grandparent possible, she says, you must offer emotional, spiritual, physical, and financial support to your grandchild's family.

"With mothers in the workforce and the decrease in men's real wages, the strain on families is greater now," says Bowman. "And when you throw in divorce, family life is more stressful than it was a generation ago. Young families need more support and help from grandparents than the previous generation did. They need someone to baby-sit, to pick up diapers, to sometimes give them money. It's more than just being nice. It's being helpful."

The two biggest factors in determining the roles and involvement you'll play as a grandparent in a stable family are your time and your relationship with the young parents.

> **Sue (Nana) Crawford:** *"I'm real bad about saying no when it comes to baby-sitting. I don't speak up. There isn't any real reason why I can't. Just because I don't want to [baby-sit] isn't a good enough reason."*

You should talk things out with the new parents—the sooner the better—and try to fashion an understanding, says Bowman. "One grandparent might say, 'I can sit one day a week,' another will say, 'Whenever you need me, call me.' It depends on your relationship with your kids. Most parents know their children pretty well by the time they start having babies of their own. As a general rule, the more specific grandparents and parents can be about roles, the better."

But be diplomatic and respectful when talking with the young parents, says Dr. Buffington. "If you come right out during the pregnancy and say, 'This is what I will do and won't do,' without really discussing things, it won't work. Hormones are coursing through their veins and they'll take it as a direct affront. Explain in what ways you can help them and then tell them your time limitations in a very positive fashion."

> **Nana Jo:** *"My daughter got her self-esteem from her job. I hear things like, 'I didn't go to college to change diapers.' Child-rearing is unfulfilling to her in some ways so I don't think she'll be a stay-at-home mom for much longer. I do some things for her that I don't really want to do just to take the pressure off of her so she'll stay home longer with the children."*

Says Dr. Susan Ginsberg, "To make grandparenting work, you have to set parameters and have some realistic expectations on both sides. Like many boomer grandparents, you probably have obligations other than work and family. Tell your adult child: 'I will do what I can' and then make sure you follow through.

"So much has to do with the way your adult children respond to you. What is their expectation of you? Are they going to lay the guilt on you and put you in positions where you have to say no to them because you are working? Boomers are not the stereotypical grandparents of old who have lots of time on their hands. That's what your children have to get used to. You have a life."

> **Linda (Mimi) Gray:** *"I'm more than just a grandmother. I am a wife, a mother, a businesswoman, a church worker, a volunteer, a tennis player. I love my kids and grandchild dearly, but I have a life of my own to lead."*

If you weren't around as much as you should have been when your kids were growing up, having your first grandchild can spur you to become a new person. Maybe you were getting Vinnie Barbarino grades in parenting. Well, here's your opportunity to transform yourself and change your family's perception of you. "When you become a grandparent, you can reinvent yourself," says Dr. Buffington. "You can absolve yourself of all your failures as a parent and start all over when you're with your grandkids."

Many of us change without making a conscious effort to do so, he says. "There is something neat about male and female roles as you age. Many of us fit stereotypical feminine and masculine roles until we hit about fifty and then those roles reverse. Where women were more emotional, they become more analytical and men become more emotional and nurturing. That's why you see this hard-hitting CEO who, when he becomes fifty, turns into a doting grandfather. He doesn't know it, but God just played a cheap hormonal trick on him.

"As you age, you become more other-centered rather than self-centered. It's wonderful. Especially if you have achieved what you want in life and if you are where you want to be. Grandparenting is like a swan song. It's your last official family role. It's your gift to the world."

Whatever grandparenting roles you choose, be true to yourself and respect your needs. Don't feel guilty if they don't match up to the expectations of others, says Dr. Buffington. "The best, age-old, trite advice in the world is to approach any differences with your adult children over your role as honestly as you can. Be as straight as you can and compromise the best that you can. If you do, you have no reason to be afraid or ashamed for taking charge of your life."

> **Keri (Grams) Lytle:** *"My grandmother said things like, 'No matter what you say or do, make sure your kids smell nice,' and 'Don't let the kids go barefoot until after the first of May.' I hope my grandchildren don't expect me to come up with sayings like that."*

In her book, *Innovative Grandparenting*, author and grandmother Karen O'Connor writes:

> We can be who we are right now. Stereotypes are out. Individuals are in. You can be who you are and still be a "great" grandmother or grandfather—whether you live in a trailer or a tent in a condo or a cottage in a hotel or a house.
>
> The important things haven't changed, namely the presence of a grandparent in the life of a child, your presence in the life of your grandchildren.

If we are to avoid the stereotypes and enjoy our grandparenting years without guilt and without the imposition of others' standards, it will be important to know who we are and who we are not, what we are willing to do and what we are unwilling to do.

I feel certain of one thing. It's okay, in fact it's important and necessary, for each of us to have a life apart from grandparenting. We need definition and purpose beyond our role in the life of our children and grandchildren. We were on earth before them, and they are likely to be here long after we're gone, so it's not healthy to cling to them for our identity.

Doing the Hustle

Dealing with full-time work, outside activities, and personal needs while still maintaining a close relationship with your grandchild can turn your life into a twenty-four-hour-a-day Latin Hustle.

"When my daughter gave birth in Boston, I raced up from New York to see her in the hospital and then I had to race back to New York because I had to make a presentation at a conference," Dr. Ginsberg recalls. "I'm not as available as I'd like. I don't have the flexibility as the grandmother who doesn't work. I admit I have grandmother guilt. I'm aware you shouldn't feel guilty about things you can't control. That's good advice, but not always effective.

"Sometimes it depends on the kind of support your adult child has. In my case, I have a daughter whose mother-in-law doesn't work. She's there, she's available, and she's wonderful. That takes the onus off of me a little bit.

"You need to set priorities and manage your time. For example, there is a Grandparents' Day at my granddaughter's school. There would have to be a very serious business obligation to keep me away. That's a priority. I go and I love it."

Your grandparenting role will be as important to you as the time you are willing to spend on it, says Bowman. "It's a choice a grandparent has to make. If you aren't willing to baby-sit your grandchild or have him over for the weekend, you're not going to have the same level of intimacy with him that you'll have if you get to put him to bed only occasionally."

In her own family, the grandparents still work. "But we're at the stage in our careers where we're more flexible in our work time. I have less and less concern about taking time out to do things with my granddaughter."

> **Nana on the Net:** *"When I'm going to have my beautiful grand-daughter Jenna, I make sure my schedule is clear. No work, no appointments, no chores. I clear my day to give her total 'grandma' time."*

Dr. Buffington believes there are many boomer grandparents who can juggle their work, their volunteer efforts, and other activities and still be good nanas and papas. That's usually because they already have figured out their roles.

He adds, "Ideally, we should create in our minds a mission statement: 'This is what I will do in my life.' Then set priorities. Look at the things you enjoy and ask yourself which you like more—golf, bridge, whatever, or spending time with your grandkids. Then make the appropriate decision. Do you have to spend extra time at work that keeps you away from your grandkids? Sometimes your financial situation gives you no choice. You have to work. That's the nature of the beast and you shouldn't feel guilty about it. That's just the way it is. But sometimes it isn't that way. You need to really examine your life."

Dr. Kornhaber believes in maintaining a balance between your personal life, your work, and family responsibilities. "Many families are reexamining their priorities, and grandparents are seeking to balance their lives more effectively," he says. "Grandfathers today are beginning to understand that their role affords them an opportunity to be with children, something that this new generation of grandfathers had little time for in their younger days as parents.

"I've often taken a day off of my practice and spent it with the grandkids. This is what I mean by balance. A lot of us have jobs that allow us to do that. I'm going to balance my life because the babies are so cute for the first several years. I want to be there because the babies go crazy when they see their grandparents. I want to savor that time in life. That's where the concept of balance comes in. I don't have to be a sixty-hour-per-week work drone. I can pull back a little. I want to spend a little more time with the grandchildren and give the parents a break too."

Multiple Roles

Your grandparenting role will evolve as your life and the needs of your family change.

"Do the best you can," suggests Bowman. "If you keep working at it, it gets better. There are times when the needs and demands of the grandchildren conflict with those of the grandparents and there's no easy way to get around that except through family discussion.

"The best piece of advice I can give is have the adult child be willing to be a parent. It works best when your child carries out the parenting role well and leaves you free to figure out the grandparenting role. When the parenting role isn't being well implemented, it makes it very difficult to be the kind of grandparent you want to be."

An increasing number of boomer nanas and papas are involved in the daily care of their grandchildren from day one—not necessarily by choice but by necessity (a subject discussed in more detail later).

"As the family structure changes, boomer grandparents need to adapt," says Dr. Buffington. "We are seeing more grandparents involved in helping to raise the kids because there are so many single parents who work. The grandparent, usually the grandmother, takes care of the kid during the day because she's cheaper and more trustworthy than other forms of day care. But that's a two-edged sword. You are a parent by day and a grandparent by night. For many, the grandparenting role is evolving into a direct parenting role, which could cause problems in the long run. They are acting more like parents than grandparents.

"But you must be there for your family. You give them a safety net of stability in times of crisis. Sometimes you just need to lend a hand. That's what families do."

The boomer generation is also the sandwich generation. We're the first to see, in large-scale numbers, our parents become great-grandparents. Because of medical advances and healthier living, the fastest-growing segment of the U.S. population are those people over the age of eighty-five.

Grandparents whose parents are still living often face a dilemma. "If you don't already, you'll have multiple caregiving roles," says Dr. Peter Martin. "You are involved in your adult children's and grandchildren's lives as well as your parents'. Who is going to provide for your parents' needs? Where are they going to live? When are you going to visit them? Are you going to have the time and money to fly to Kansas City to see the grandkids and then go on to Arizona to visit your parents?"

> **Sue (Nana) Crawford:** *"I'm part of the sandwich generation so I spend a lot of time helping my mother and [Sue's daughter] Chrisy with the two kids. I don't have time for me. When I go to our beach house, that's my escape. When I'm gone, they fend for themselves because they can do it. I still feel that sense of responsibility to Chrisy to try and make things easier because she's still my kid."*

Be aware that as your parents become more dependent on you, the whole family will be affected. Time and energy will be taken away from your role as a spouse, parent, and grandparent in order to meet the needs of your elderly parents.

"Baby boomers need to be talking to their elderly parents before an emergency or crisis occurs," says Sandy Markwood, CEO of the National Association of Area Agencies on Aging. "Unfortunately, most adult children are ill-prepared for when their parents get sick and face these issues."

It might not be easy to discuss financial, legal, and health issues with your aging parents, but you need to be prepared. It will help you and your family when a crisis erupts. For a guide with advice and a checklist of questions to discuss with your parents, go to www.eldercare.gov. The site also features Eldercare Locator, a free service that links families to local aging resources.

Adds Dr. Susan Ginsberg, "When you have older parents, more crises come up quickly that you must respond to. It can be hard, especially if your children or grandchildren need you. That's when you must get other relatives to share the responsibility. You can't be expected to take care of four generations by yourself.

"Adjust your expectations and don't have a fantasy of being Superman or Superwoman. Take it one day at a time and know that there likely will be hard times ahead."

Sherry (Grammy) Johnson: *"The grandkids help me sometimes with their great-grandparents. It's a life struggle-juggle."*

The Role of Great-Grandparents

It's estimated that half of today's grandparents will eventually become great-grandparents. According to a University of Southern California study, between 1970 and 2000, there has been a tenfold increase in the number of great-grandparents who are actively involved in the lives of their great-grandchildren.

So where do the great-grandparents fit in the family picture?

"It depends on their vitality," says Dr. Kornhaber. "If great-grandparents are still somewhat active and in good health, then they become the number-one icon in their family. They don't necessarily have the role as nurturers but they can certainly function as living ancestors and family historians. They can give children firsthand accounts of life in another time. They are the family archivists, providing grandchildren with a link to the past through stories of relatives long dead."

Great-grandparents are living symbols who provide a sense of family roots and a new perspective for children in understanding the past, present, and future.

Seventy-seven-year-old Mira (Baba) Mrantz: *"Great-grandparenting is better than grandparenting. It feels wonderful because I have watched the lives of my grandchildren from the day they were born to their graduations, weddings, and the birth of their children.*

"The family is looking up to me and makes me feel I am the empress. It's an incredible feeling. They realize I am running out of time. And they are paying a lot of attention to me.

"I don't offer much parenting advice. My daughter raised her children pretty much the way I raised her. It's being passed on.

Whenever I say to my grandchildren, 'You're doing such a nice job of raising your children,' they turn around and say, 'If it hadn't been for you, we wouldn't be who we are.' That makes me feel good.

"It's important for me to be in constant touch with the great-grandbabies so they know who I am and where they come from. They know who I am because they talk to me on the phone all the time and I see them every few months. We are very close. Just to hear their voices makes my day. If I don't hear their voices after a few days, I go bananas. I just hope I will be around to see the great-grandchildren grow up."

"Involve the great-grandparents as long as you can," urges Dr. Buffington. "They are a joy from heaven." When a child talks to his great-grandparents, he is, in essence, connecting with perhaps six generations—his own, his parents', his grandparents', and his great-grandparents', and through their firsthand accounts about his great-great- and great-great-great grandparents'.

"The great-grandparent serves as the trunk of the family tree," says Dr. Gregory Sanders. "It's a living trunk, and all those branches are tied together by that person. We usually don't think about establishing relationships with distant cousins, but when you have that living connection, there's more pride in the family and more of an opportunity to get together and make connections. There are cousins and second cousins twice removed who would not normally be gathering together if they hadn't had a connection with that elderly person."

If you haven't already, get your parents or other elderly relatives in front of a video camera, DVD recorder, or tape recorder and start pumping them for family stories and anecdotes before it's too late. For that matter, plop yourself down in front of the camera and start reminiscing about your childhood, like the time you threw up on Mr. Wizard's TV show or got a ride in the Weinermobile.

"Increased age means increased time to mature and accumulate family history and to serve as a living ancestor for more people," says Dr. Kornhaber. "With their storehouse full of wisdom and experience, great-grandparents can have an even greater potential positive influence than they had as grandparents."

The New Grandparent

Allan: *"I was blown away when I held Chad for the first time. I don't know if I was shell-shocked from realizing I was now a grandfather or from realizing that my firstborn child was now a mother."*

Michelle (Grammy) Davies: *"When I first saw my grandson, I thought, 'Oh, goody, I finally have someone I can spoil rotten.'"*

Keri (Grams) Lytle: *"I will never forget the feeling I had holding [her granddaughter] Maddie just minutes after her birth. It was indescribable joy and wonder. I bawled almost as loudly as she did."*

Actor Billy Crystal, upon becoming a grandfather for the first time: *"I'm on cloud ten. I can see cloud nine from here."*

WHEN YOU BECOME A NEW GRANDPARENT, go ahead and tell the world. Burn up the phone lines and plaster the Internet with pictures of the baby. Or you could outdo some of your fellow boomers. When their grandson was three months old, a Dallas couple sent out five dozen invitations for a "sip 'n see"—basically a showing, accompanied by wine and cheese, of their grandchild. New grandparents in Milwaukee threw a "baby beer bash" to introduce the newest member of the family. We've even heard of new nanas and papas who took out ads in their local newspaper announcing the birth of their grandchild.

To Be (There), Or Not to Be (There)

Where will you be (or where were you) at the birth of your grandchild? In the waiting room? In the birthing room? At home or at work waiting for the phone call? (We're not talking about the boomers whose grand-children were born in the bathroom of a 747, in a crowded subway, next to the dairy case of a convenience store, or on the wedding altar—all of which really happened.)

Whether or not it's your first grandchild, to fully appreciate this most profound of experiences, you really need to be there at the birth, says Dr. Arthur Kornhaber. "The new mother and father are giving their parents a gift of a child. It's very important that the grandparents are there to receive that gift."

Boomer dads were the first fathers on a large scale to gain admit-tance into the delivery room beginning in the '70s. Now our genera-tion is banging on the door to let family and friends share in the blessed event. Today an increasing number of boomer grandparents are attending the birth of their grandchild or are standing right outside the door during the delivery.

"The birth of a new family member is a momentous experience," says Dr. Kornhaber. "The happiness, fulfillment, and spiritual joy that every baby brings reach far beyond the mother and father to resonate within the hearts of all family members.

"When I delivered babies, I had grandmothers come into the room. It's the most incredible experience. It's so powerful the room lights up. You remember in the movie when Charlton Heston, as Moses, went up the mountain and came down with white hair? That's what it's like."

> **Peggy (Granma) Minacci:** *"There were fourteen of us standing outside the delivery room. Right after Michael Thomas was born, my son David came out. He walked through the crowd with this big smile and everyone parted so he could get to my husband Ken and hug him. It was such a moving experience. The family calls it 'The Happening.'"*

Not everyone thinks grandparents should be attending the birth. "Watch the video," says Dr. Perry Buffington. "I grew up on a farm and saw animals giving birth all the time. My grandfather used to say to all of us who were watching, 'Don't crowd the animal.' That's good advice. There are some things that should be between a man and wife, and I don't know why you want a family reunion in the delivery room. It's an intimate, bonding moment for the parents. Only so many people can cut that cord anyway. Certainly, if the parents want the grandparents in there, fine. But don't show up expecting to walk right in. Wait for an invitation from the parents-to-be, and if you don't get one, just live with it."

Dr. Kornhaber's Foundation for Grandparenting has been championing the cause for nanas and papas to attend the birth of their grandchildren. "However," he admits, "we still find a great deal of reluctance on the part of many families to do this. Many reasons are given. One young mother wanted only her husband with her in the delivery room. A grandmother-to-be said, 'I know my daughter-in-law would rather be with her own mother at a time like this.' A nurse told us, 'I can't have the whole family in the delivery room. It isn't sanitary.' One grandfather complained, 'I can't leave work.' These arguments, plausible as they be, miss the point. Of course people are modest, families are different, and everyone's busy. Indeed, hospital policy may work against our good intentions.

"No one is saying that Grandma and Grandpa have to be looking over the doctor's shoulder when the baby comes. Grandma, for example, could be in the delivery room and Grandpa outside the door until the delivery is over. Then he could hold the baby, say hello, and place the first teddy bear in the baby's arms. The point is that grandparents should be there to welcome the baby, thank the new parents for the gift of the child, and offer to help in any way necessary—and most of all to share the joy."

> **Sandy Smith:** *"I got to watch my daughter give birth to my grandson. It was the most wonderful experience of my life—even more than having my own children."*

Carolynn Bauer Zorn, who witnessed the birth of four of her grandchildren and is the author of *Attending Your Grandchild's Birth*, encourages grandparents to be in the delivery room. "When you attend the birth of your grandchild, the birth event becomes a rite of passage where everyone celebrates the addition of a new generation to the family. Your children become parents and you become grandparents. You all move up a branch on the family tree. It is an emotional and spiritual event that touches everyone in attendance. Sharing your grandchild's birth provides unforgettable memories."

If grandparents are present, they can relieve the new dad of taking pictures or operating the video camera so he can be more responsive and focused on the mother, not to mention that he'll appear in all the pictures with his wife and new baby. Besides, adds Zorn, grandparents are more likely to take pictures for all to see, unlike a zealous husband whose photography of that magical moment might be more revealing than the new mom cares to share with others.

Also, says Zorn, grandparents can offer needed support during an urgent situation. "Decisions can be daunting if the husband has to make them alone. An understanding and supportive family can be a great help if they are present when an emergency occurs."

Charles Hersch: *"We waited anxiously [outside the delivery room]. And then we heard the sound—the baby's first cry, surely one of the most thrilling and profound experiences of my life. It truly stands alone, and I am so grateful for having been there. The baby was brought out and passed around. While that was wonderful, it did not equal the shock of that first sound, the sudden realization that our grandchild was really here. If you have the opportunity to experience what we did, I would enthusiastically urge you to seize it."*

Boomer grandmother Dr. Anya Luchow Liberman, a family psychologist and a member of the grandparents.com panel of experts, believes it's important for the mother of the new mother to be present at the birth. "This is a mother-daughter thing. The mother-in-law shouldn't be offended. I wouldn't expect my daughter-in-law to want me in there with her. There's a level of intimacy that, no matter how close you are with someone else, is different between a mother and daughter. Mom knows what it's like to give birth and knows how to comfort her child. You are sharing that moment with your daughter, which is an amazing experience, an awe-inspiring moment of connection.

"I was in the delivery room when my two daughters gave birth, and it was a magical experience for me both times. I have been telling the daughter of every friend of mine that the biggest gift she can give her mother is to let her be present at the birth."

Dr. T. Berry Brazelton believes the decision to include the grandparents should be left solely up to the new parents. "I don't see any problem with my being there, but my children might. It's such an individual choice. The birth is a time for enhancing the self-image of the young parents. Personally I think it would be wonderful if all three generations were celebrating in the event. This is how the Mayans did it. Everybody participated, everybody groaned when the mother had a labor pain."

Carrie (Maw Maw) Dulcette: *"My daughter Shannon had an at-home birth in a tub attended by a midwife. Shannon invited her family and friends over for the delivery. We had a party in the living room and people wandered in and out, checking on Shannon. As soon as the baby was born, we popped champagne and toasted my grandson Sean."*

We weren't there for the birth of our first grandchild, Chad. So when our daughter Allison was pregnant with our second grandchild, Danny, we asked her if we could be in the delivery room for his birth. She turned us down flat.

"I want it to be just [her husband] Dan and me," she explained. "I'd like you right outside the delivery room so you can hear what's going on. Then ten minutes later, after the baby and I are cleaned up, you can come in. Those ten minutes will make up precious bonding time between Dan, the baby, and me. It's such a personal thing between a husband and wife—and I want to keep it that way."

We were at the hospital when Allison was about to give birth to Danny. In fact, we were allowed in the delivery room during labor. We had hoped that everyone would be so preoccupied they would forget about our presence. But then we learned the true meaning of the phrase "when push comes to shove." When Allison began to push, the nurse began to shove us out.

We stood outside in the hall, each pressing an ear against the door, straining to hear every word and sound in the delivery room. (Next time, we'll each bring a stethoscope or at least a drinking glass to help us hear through the door.)

Allan: *"When we heard Danny's first wails, tears of happiness trickled down our faces. Here was a new precious gift of life; a new member of our family to love; a new cherished grandson. But we couldn't help notice that the baby's initial cries sounded like frantic quacks. 'My God,' gasped Kathryn, 'Allison gave birth to a duck!'*

"We laughed and hugged until Dan, the proud dad, came out to announce that mother and baby were doing great. Moments later, we introduced ourselves to Danny, who was no longer quacking and seemed quite content with his new surroundings.

"Once Kathryn—a.k.a. 'the baby hog'—entered the room, Allison and Dan didn't get to hold Danny very much. I have a feeling that if Kathryn had been there for the actual delivery, she would have grabbed the baby right out of the doctor's arms before the umbilical cord was even cut."

Kathryn: *"Even though I wished I had witnessed the births of each of our grandchildren, I wouldn't have wanted my parents with me when I delivered our daughters. Giving birth is an emotional and physical experience that you can't fully describe unless you've been through it. You never forget it, even when you start those midlife memory lapses. I never felt closer to each of my babies or my husband than I did at those times. They were such deep, wonderful, intimate minutes shared by mom, dad, and baby and no one else—a moment in time to be cherished and savored by only the three of us.*

"So I understand Allison's decision. Although I'd still jump at the chance to be in the delivery room, I'm okay with being outside the door. I don't feel hurt or left out. This is a time for the three of them. This is not a time for Nana. There will be plenty of Nana times. Who knows? Maybe when our other daughter,

*Sasha, gets pregnant, she'll want me in the delivery room. If so,
I'll be there in a flash."*

Allison's friends reported a wide range of experiences about having
the grandparents-to-be attend a birth. Recalls Allison:

"Kayce had her parents in there. Her mom and dad each held one
of her legs while her husband held her hand. She wouldn't have it any
other way. She loved having her mom and dad in there.

"It was different for Mitzi and for Amy. In both cases, their parents
were with them until the contractions started getting bad, then the
girls wanted the parents out of there. The parents got upset seeing
their kids in pain and that made Mitzi and Amy more nervous and
uncomfortable.

"Regan had her husband and mom in there with her. Regan loved
it and her mom did too because her mom had been knocked out when
Regan was born. But this time her mom finally got to see a birth, and it
was a glorious experience for her.

"Another friend wanted to have her parents with her, but she felt
uncomfortable having her in-laws in there. She knew that would be a
big problem, so she decided against having any of them with her for
the birth.

"Then there was Fran. She had eleven people in the delivery room
for her second baby. They were all in the room during labor and when
it came time for her to push, they said, 'We'll get out.' She said, 'If you
all want to stay, you can. I've had an epidural and I feel great!' She was
covered up. So she had her mom, in-laws and friends—all women—
there and they loved it. All she asked was that there be no pictures
taken of her until she had a chance to put on makeup five minutes
after the birth. She looked absolutely beautiful in the photos."

Jane (Grandmom) Whitfield: *"My daughter-in-law Chollet
involved her mother, stepmother, and me throughout her pregnancy. We were there [for the sonogram] when she discovered she
was going to have a boy. We were all tickled. For the birth, a whole
batch of us were outside the delivery room in the hall. It was three
A.M. when we heard the baby cry. About a half hour later, we all*

paraded in. Chollet's mother got to hold the baby first, then me, then her stepmother. It sort of went in a pecking order."

Home or Away?

When Allison gave birth to Chad, we headed to their home in Tallahassee. We couldn't wait to see and hold our new grandson. During the eight-hour drive, we had visions of entering a happy house where two beaming young parents would be cooing at their new son; the rooms would be brimming with festive balloons, flowers, and cards; and we would be spending idle, contented hours admiring the newest member of the family. Yeah, right, and Nixon was blameless for Watergate.

Kathryn: "I walked into the house and immediately grabbed for the baby while practically ignoring my daughter who had just gone through a tremendous emotional and physical experience. She was suffering from postpartum blues, excessive bleeding, and engorgement. She was in pain and exhausted. The baby was crying and our son-in-law Dan felt helpless and stressed out. Meanwhile, I was concentrating all my love and attention on the baby.

"But then it dawned on me that Allison needed mothering more than Chad needed grandmothering at this point. I changed the focus of my visit and began taking care of Allison. I tended to her needs, and those of her family—preparing meals, doing the laundry and ironing, and cleaning the house. It was hard for me to watch the new parents struggling through those post-pregnancy problems. Fortunately, within a couple of days, everything had worked out. It was still hard for me, though. I am a 'baby hog' by nature, but I had to stand back and let the baby and his parents get better acquainted. Chad belonged to Allison and Dan—and they had first dibs."

Should you stay at the new parents' house right after the birth of your grandchild? It depends. If you're going there solely to see the baby and be entertained, get a hotel room. If you plan on helping out in any way you can, maybe you should remain with them. But it's up to the new parents.

Dr. Brazelton says he and his wife never stayed in the home of their children right after a birth. "I thought that was intrusive. We stayed in a nearby hotel. We'd go over during the day and do whatever we could to help out. My wife did all the housework. What surprised me was how much our children needed our physical help.

"As a grandparent, you should support the new parents as much as they will let you. It's a very vulnerable time, and if you are there offering advice and intruding, it could really upset the apple cart. You have to be extra respectful of the stress that parents are under. To be available without being intrusive is a very important role for new grandparents."

Lisa O'Cain: *"My daughter asked us to wait for two weeks before flying to Chicago to see them. They wanted to be totally alone. Do you know how hard that was for me? I was worried sick about her and I was way too impatient to see my first grandchild—and there was nothing I could do about it."*

Jane (Grandmom) Whitfield: *"[Her son] Mark and [daughter-in-law] Chollet didn't want anybody there because they wanted to handle things by themselves. No one spent the night with them, but I did bring over meals. The little rascal didn't sleep at all and Chollet was just worn out. She was at the point where she wasn't sure this motherhood was all that great. I remember how worn out I was when I was a new mother. I called Chollet and said, 'If there's anything I can do, I'll be there in a minute.' But they managed to handle it on their own."*

Sue (Nana) Crawford: *"I flew up right after the baby was born and stayed with them. I slept on the living room sofa for five nights and went to the grocery store and cooked. [Her daughter] Chrisy wanted me there like yesterday because she was having a difficult time at first. I wish I had arrived before the baby was born."*

Taking a small informal poll of new mothers, we found that virtually all said they wanted and needed help during the baby's first few days at home. They suggested that grandparents can make life easier during this time by:

- not voicing your opinions, unless asked, about the choice of the baby's name
- respecting the new mother's need to bond with her child
- accepting, without comment, the parents' wishes to follow their methods of baby care even if they're different than what you followed as a young parent
- being sensitive, supportive, and understanding of the new parents
- asking what you can do to help—and then doing it, such as handling the chores and running errands
- bringing over food that requires little or no preparation and is easy to clean up
- offering to look after any other children in the family for a few hours (or possibly a few days)
- getting along with the other grandparents and not competing with them for attention

If possible, try to fashion an understanding with the young couple before the birth about your immediate role. That way, everyone in the family will know his or her responsibilities and expectations when the baby comes home.

Here's what several new mothers had to say about having the grandparents around:

> **Bekka Bailey:** *"It was a little too much having relatives there because I was an emotional and physical wreck and I felt I had to entertain them. I just wanted Mom and Dad to cook for me and take care of the house and do my dirty work. I didn't want my relatives to see me that way. If they had come a week later, it would have been better."*

> **Stephanie Alterton:** *"For the first baby, you definitely need someone to stay with you—your mom, a sister, a good friend,*

*whoever you feel close to. For the second baby, I'd love for some-
one to come a month before and a month after."*

Anna Bowen: *"Most of my friends wanted their mothers because
they felt more comfortable with them. Some friends didn't want their
fathers there because they didn't want their daddies to see them in
that kind of state. Moms are used to it, some dads aren't."*

For the birth of your son's or daughter's second child, the focus of
your visit should be on caring for the first grandchild. There will be
plenty for you to do without being in the way. Typically, the parents
are more confident and relaxed and know what to expect during the
first few days home with the second child, so you can focus more on
your first grandchild.

When you arrive, bring a special gift just for him, make him the center of attention, and keep him entertained, allowing Mom to concentrate
on caring for the baby. Spend as much time as possible with the first
grandchild, even if it means getting up early to quietly fix breakfast for
him and the rest of the family so Mom can sleep between feedings.

Kathryn: *"Because Allan and I had flexible schedules, we arrived
at Allison's and Dan's home a week before Danny's birth. I'm
glad we did because we were able to run errands and do chores so
that Allison, who was very tired and very uncomfortable, could
get some rest.*

*"We were better able to chase after Chad, who was almost
two years old at the time, and play with him. It took us a couple
of days to get down his routine—including playgroup, nap time,
bath time, and bedtime. We also had time to learn 'Chad-speak.'
(We finally figured out that 'Ah duh' meant 'All done.') By the
time Allison went into the hospital to give birth, she was well-
rested and had a smooth delivery. And we were getting along
great with Chad.*

*"When Allison returned home with Danny, we made the
arrival a fun time for Chad. When he wasn't holding and kissing
his little brother, he was spending hours with his nana and papa*

blowing bubbles, looking at picture books, making sidewalk chalk drawings, playing in the sandbox, and frolicking with the hose. He had such a good time that he didn't show any jealousy or competition for his mother's affection.

"To put it simply: If a two-year-old is happy, everyone is happy."

The best way to help the family, Dr. Brazelton contends, is to fall in love with the baby. "I always say every baby needs at least one person, preferably two, who are passionately in love with him or her. When it gets to be two or more, isn't that baby even luckier?"

Adoptive and Special Needs Grandchildren

Becoming a grandparent to an adoptive or special needs child can be challenging, but also very enriching and rewarding.

"I cannot emphasize enough how important it is to be supportive and sensitive to what the parents are experiencing," says Dr. Kornhaber. "The process and logistics of adoption can create very specific tensions in family relationships."

Once the decision is made and the process begins, it helps if you join the fun and preparation of awaiting the arrival of your new grandchild. Instead of seeing him for the first time at a hospital maternity ward, it might be at an airport. Instead of being a newborn infant, he might be a toddler or even older. Instead of being a spitting image of you or your adult child, he might be of a different or mixed race.

If the parents adopted internationally, you get the opportunity to be a member of a transcultural and/or transracial family. You get to learn new traditions and customs that will have resonance and meaning in your life. You might celebrate not only Thanksgiving but also Chuseok, the Korean equivalent; not only April Fool's Day but also the Day of the Innocents, the Guatemalan equivalent.

If having a grandchild who looks so different than you stretches your boundaries of understanding and tolerance, remember this: He is connected to you and to his family, and although he may not look like anyone in the family, he likely will develop similar voice patterns, talents, tastes, and interests. And remember one other thing: He deserves your love and support.

"Some grandparents report feeling a bit strange with their adopted grandchild at first, but the more time they spend with the child, the closer they feel," says Dr. Kornhaber.

It can be even more difficult for a grandparent if the adopted child is developmentally challenged, suffers a disability, is a victim of war, or a crack baby. "If you are having trouble with this issue, try not to blame yourself or feel guilty," says Dr. Kornhaber. "Do, however, consult a trusted friend, counselor, or member of the clergy. Talk the issue through and try to resolve things in your mind. Above all, work toward preserving and nurturing your relationship to your new grandchild."

When a baby is born with special needs, it can be especially challenging for the entire family. In such a case, grandparents can offer indispensable help to their grandchild and the parents. "Everyone involved with the child's care—from doctors to parents—needs to understand how to access the helping and healing power of grandparents," says Dr. Kornhaber. "No matter what the problem is, that child wants to love and be loved, to grow, to learn, to have freedom, and to have fun."

Learn as much as you can about your grandchild's condition. Talk to his doctor and parents of other children with the same affliction; read everything you can on the subject and understand what medical science can and can't do.

Discuss the situation with the parents and decide how best you can help. "For example," says Dr. Kornhaber, "many grandparents help financially. Others are involved in the child's daily treatment routine, which might include such tasks as doing exercises with a physically handicapped grandchild on a daily basis or helping out with a remedial learning program."

He also suggests that you tune in carefully to the parents' emotional, mental, and physical health. Be willing to give them respite or comfort. "In such difficult circumstances, you are indispensable to your grandchild and to your children. Your emotional leadership and physical involvement will help you grow and learn, bring your family closer, and set a positive example for future generations of grandparents in your family."

They Don't Do It That Way Anymore

Boomer offspring prepare for parenthood as if they are going for their master's degree. They huddle with pediatricians, obstetricians, lactation consultants, midwives, labor and delivery nurses, and birthing coaches. Never mind how many children *you* raised; in their eyes, you probably know as much about today's baby care trends as Ralph Kramden knew about personal conflict resolution. Baby care is different now.

That was then: As young parents, we put our babies on their stomachs at night.

This is now: Medical experts agree that babies should sleep on their backs or sides to lessen the risk of Sudden Infant Death Syndrome.

That was then: Our doctors encouraged us to follow a schedule of feedings for our babies.

This is now: Today, physicians realize such schedules aren't practical or necessary because babies' hunger varies depending on activity and growth. Babies have a natural hunger drive. They know when they are hungry and when they are full.

That was then: It was common practice to give babies solid food within four to six weeks after birth.

This is now: Most experts agree that six weeks is way too early to start even simple foods like cereal. A baby's stomach and intestines aren't developed enough to handle solid foods before at least four to six months. At that age they can be introduced to rice cereal. The current thinking for breast-fed babies is not to wean them for a year.

That was then: We were cautioned that responding too quickly and too often to our babies' cries would spoil them.

This is now: For the first few months of life, at least, a baby cannot be spoiled, experts claim. She's not crying with the intention of manipulating her parents; she's crying because she's trying to communicate. When her parents respond promptly and lovingly to her crying, they're building her trust and encouraging her development. She's learning that the people around her love and care for her.

That was then: We kept a bottle of ipecac syrup on hand to induce vomiting in case children ingested something poisonous.

This is now: The American Academy of Pediatrics (AAP) has reversed its long-standing position and now recommends that parents call poison control centers when children ingest toxic substances.

That was then: We put our babies to sleep on waterbeds, sheep-skin, soft mattresses, pillows, quilts and comforters, and in cribs loaded with stuffed toys.

This is now: The AAP says parents should never place infants on top of soft, fluffy bedding because it can become molded around the babies' faces and suffocate them. Parents should put infants under twelve months on their backs in a crib with a firm, tight-fitting mattress. Use a sleeper or other sleep clothing as an alternative to blankets with no other covering. If using a blanket, put the baby with her feet at the foot of the crib. Tuck a thin blanket around the crib mattress only as far as the baby's chest.

Mini Milestones

Can you remember when your kids said their first words, or took their first steps, or cut their first teeth? We couldn't with our kids either (although we do remember the exact date when we saw the Beatles perform at old Comiskey Park in Chicago—August 20, 1965).

Fuzzy memories from your early parenting days make it difficult to know when to anticipate your grandchild's developmental milestones. To help you, here's a little primer on what to expect of a typical child during the first five years of life. This guide also includes ways that experts say you can enhance your grandchild's development.

Keep this in mind: Children are individuals with their own internal clocks that ring when they are ready to walk, talk, and dress themselves. It's unfair to compare the development of one child with another.

Throughout your grandchild's early development, you should interact with her as often as you can. That means hug, cuddle, and rock her; talk, sing, and read to her—and, above all, just love her and have fun!

The Infant

Your grandchild is learning to trust in someone who can be counted on for care, fun, protection, and limits. She's discovering her physical abilities and the new things around her. When her needs are met and she receives loving care in a stable environment, she gains trust in her new world.

Her sense of touch develops rapidly, and it's one she enjoys. According to a University of Miami study, the more babies are picked up, hugged, and massaged, the better they develop. Babies who are touched frequently sleep better and have faster-developing nervous systems than do other babies.

Singing, cooing, and talking to your infant grandchild will encourage her to imitate the sounds she hears. Good hearing is the key to language development.

At 0–3 Months

Your grandchild likely will:

- lift her head
- follow a slowly-moving object with her eyes
- laugh
- smile
- bring her hands together
- love to be touched
- see best when things are eight to twelve inches away (the distance of a nursing baby from her mother's face) because her sight is about 20/200.

What you can do for your grandchild:

- Take every opportunity to massage her. Apply some pressure during the massage and use a small amount of baby oil to help your hands glide over her skin.
- Enjoy having her touch you back. Babies are comforted by laying their hands on others' hands and faces.
- Wear clothes with contrasting light-dark patterns. She prefers sights that have high contrast.
- Give support for her immature neck muscles when you're holding her.
- Buy stimulating toys for her to see and hear. Some good choices: a simple mobile for over the crib; an unbreakable, smooth-edged mirror attached to the side of the crib; a music box; and a prism to hang in the nursery window.
- Provide plenty of physical contact.
- Hold her close to your face.
- Talk to her in a high-pitched voice. She's attuned to that tone and is capable of distinguishing human speech from other sounds.
- Wear the same lotion or fragrance each time you visit to take advantage of her keen sense of smell. She might recognize your special scent.
- Provide floor time for her in order to exercise developing muscles.
- Avoid startling her when you greet her. Approach gently and respect her own space.

At 3–6 Months

Your grandchild likely will:

- hold her head in a stable position
- bear some weight on her legs when supported in a standing position
- sit without support
- roll from her back to her stomach

- look for a dropped object
- begin eating rice cereal and unseasoned, pureed fruits and vegetables (after four months)
- show that her ability to perceive detail has improved dramatically

What you can do for your grandchild:
- Buy her a well-designed crib gym that provides objects for her to swipe at, bat, or pull; teething rings; key chains; and clutch balls that are small enough to play with and too large to be swallowed.
- Observe her interacting with her world so you can get a fascinating glimpse inside that little mind of hers.
- Keep her on the routine that she and her parents have set when it comes to eating, sleeping, and playing times.
- Introduce her to nature by putting her in a backpack and taking her for a hike. (Make sure she has adequate back and head support.)

At 6–9 Months
Your grandchild likely will:
- make an effort to get an out-of-reach toy
- pull up to a standing position from a sitting position
- hold an object
- start cutting teeth
- play simple games
- start to drink from a trainer cup that has two handles and a snap-on lid
- recognize her name
- develop the ability to judge where a sound is coming from and turn her head to locate the sound
- crawl backward or forward
- begin babbling

What you can do for your grandchild:
- Allow her to feed herself (and be prepared for the mess).
- Play games with her such as peekaboo, this little piggy, and pattycake.

- Allow her to scoot around in her bare feet whenever or wherever it's safe and comfortable.
- Give her visual stimulation. Let her see her face in a mirror, show her fish swimming in an aquarium, and always make plenty of eye contact.

At 9–12 months

Your grandchild likely will:

- walk while holding onto furniture
- stand momentarily on her own
- take her first steps
- say "mama," "dada," or other simple words at random
- start eating with a spoon
- point to body parts if asked
- climb up stairs
- learn to wave bye-bye
- enjoy undressing herself

What you can do for your grandchild:

- Baby-proof your house for a baby who can now stand and reach more things than she could before.
- Buy her bath toys, balls, books with stiff cardboard pages, and toys with uncomplicated dials, pushbuttons, and levers.

At 12–18 months

Your grandchild likely will:

- begin to walk well
- roll a ball
- begin to show some interest in toilet training
- display separation anxiety
- have her last set of toddler immunizations
- brush her teeth with a parent's help
- wear her first pair of shoes

What you can do for your grandchild:

- Offer her finger food when appropriate.
- Label objects verbally such as, "That's your teddy bear."

- Mention colors such as, "Your shirt is red."
- Provide opportunities for her to have positive experiences away from her parents by taking her to do fun things.
- Introduce her to your favorite music, particularly music with a rhythmic, repetitive beat.

The Toddler

As a toddler, your grandchild is learning to do things on her own. She's exploring her environment and testing many new skills such as talking and running. According to famed psychoanalyst Erik Erikson, this stage of life (ages two to four) is a quest for autonomy. The toddler begins to assert herself because she can walk and is talking more. She will tend to resist authority while seeking her independence as an individual.

At 18–24 Months
Your grandchild likely will:
- walk up steps
- stack blocks at least four blocks high
- name at least six body parts
- wash and dry her hands
- understand the concept of "time-out"
- use a fork

What you can do for your grandchild:
- Provide daily outdoor play whenever possible.
- Offer opportunities for active playtime such as climbing, running, kicking a ball, and pulling a wagon.

At 24–36 months
Your grandchild likely will:
- use more than fifty words
- combine words
- show an interest in playmates
- brush her teeth without help
- put on and take off her clothes by herself
- sleep in a child's bed rather than a crib

- ride a tricycle
- give up her pacifier
- be toilet trained

What you can do for your grandchild:
- Provide opportunities for one-to-one child play.
- Guide and encourage positive behaviors.
- Talk about colors, body parts, and names of familiar people.
- Praise her successes during toilet training.
- Avoid unnecessary power struggles and let her have small victories. That way, she'll have the satisfaction of feeling "I can do it."
- Provide experiences that help her explore the world around her.

The Preschooler

As a preschooler, your grandchild has formed trust and independence. Now she can move on to the more social and creative aspects of her development, which include friends and toys.

During this time, say experts, be patient and don't push her to hurry and grow up. Respect her own pace. And, oh yes, keep your sense of humor.

At age 3
Your grandchild likely will:
- use Play-Doh or crayons without putting them in her mouth
- exhibit independence and sometimes refuse to go along with adult instructions
- throw a ball overhand
- speak in two or three sentences at a time
- dress with little help
- balance on one foot briefly
- copy a circle
- prepare a bowl of cereal

- identify at least four colors
- have all twenty early childhood teeth
- not want to take a daily nap

What you can do for your grandchild:

- Provide as many "real" choices as possible such as, "Do you want to wear red socks or blue socks?"
- Encourage independence by letting her do more things for herself.
- Show her examples of good behavior, such as picking up toys together.
- Provide small motor activities to foster prewriting skills, such as molding Play-Doh, stringing beads, and tearing paper.
- Talk about letters, numbers, and colors with her.
- Teach her simple songs and nursery rhymes.
- Provide simple chores to build self-esteem, such as putting silverware away, folding washcloths, and dumping items in the trash.
- Talk to her about upcoming events and plans, for example, "Today we are going to the zoo."
- Encourage healthy habits such as brushing teeth, washing hands, exercising, and eating nutritious foods.
- Make sure she gets plenty of sleep—twelve to fourteen hours per day when she's in your care.

At age 4

Your grandchild likely will:

- prefer children to adults
- have imaginary friends
- be very active and enjoy running, jumping, and climbing
- refine her motor skills
- enjoy talking
- ask lots of questions
- have good bladder and bowel control

What you can do for your grandchild:

- Allow opportunities for her to play with other children.
- Treat her imaginary friends with respect.
- Provide crayons, markers, paint, etc.
- Be a good listener.
- Consider buying her a watch or calendar so you can mark special times and dates.
- Be understanding about occasional bladder/bowel accidents.

At age 5

Your grandchild likely will:

- begin to care about others' opinions
- display reasoning ability
- have good control of her hands and legs
- display her preference for being right- or left-handed
- be affectionate and helpful
- enjoy making new friends
- want things to be "fair"
- pretend to write or read

What you can do for your grandchild:

- Talk about feelings: happy, sad, calm, surprised.
- Give explanations and reasons for rules.
- Encourage drawing and writing—"Tell me about your picture."
- Involve her in simple, supervised cooking activities.
- Be consistent with rules, routines, and expectations.
- Point out words in the environment that she may recognize, such as McDonald's, Chuck E. Cheese, or a stop sign, etc.
- Encourage her to interact with aunts, uncles, and cousins of all ages so she has a sense of belonging to more than her immediate family.

The majority of the information on the various stages of development was adapted with permission from the Genesee County

[Michigan] Strong Families/Safe Children's *Grandparent Guidebook*. We added additional material from other child development experts.

Fifties and Sixties Songs to Sing to Your Grandchild for Fun

"(We're Gonna) Rock Around the Clock" Bill Haley and His Comets (1955)

"Hound Dog" Elvis Presley (1956)

"The Purple People Eater" Sheb Wooley (1958)

"Splish Splash" Bobby Darin (1958)

"Witch Doctor" David Seville (1958)

"Yakety Yak" The Coasters (1958)

"Shout" The Isley Brothers (1959)

"Alley-Oop" The Hollywood Argyles (1960)

"Itsy Bitsy Teenie Weenie Yellow Polkadot Bikini" Brian Hyland (1960)

"Who Put the Bomp (In the Bomp, Bomp, Bomp)" Barry Mann (1961)

"Shout! Shout! (Knock Yourself Out)" Ernie Maresca (1962)

"Surfin' Bird" The Trashmen (1963)

"Do Wha Diddy Diddy" Manfred Mann (1964)

"The Name Game" Shirley Ellis (1964)

"Wooly Bully" Sam the Sham and the Pharaohs (1965)

"I'm Henry VIII I Am" Herman's Hermits (1965)

"Wild Thing" The Troggs (1966)

"The 59th Street Bridge Song (Feelin' Groovy)" Harpers Bizarre (1967)

"Born To Be Wild" Steppenwolf (1968)

"Yummy, Yummy, Yummy" Ohio Express (1968)

"Hair" The Cowsills (1969)

Fifties and Sixties Songs to Sing to Your Grandchild at Night

"All I Have to Do Is Dream" The Everly Brothers (1958)

"Catch a Falling Star" Perry Como (1958)

"The Lion Sleeps Tonight" The Tokens (1961)

"Blowin' in the Wind" Peter, Paul and Mary (1963)

"Puff the Magic Dragon" Peter, Paul and Mary (1963)

"Deep Purple" Nino Tempo and April Stevens (1963)

"Turn! Turn! Turn! (To Everything There Is a Season)" The Byrds (1965)

"Baby, I'm Yours" Barbara Lewis (1965)

"Scarborough Fair/Canticle" Simon and Garfunkel (1966)

"Cherish" The Association (1966)

"Mellow Yellow" Donovan (1966)

"There's a Kind of Hush" Herman's Hermits (1967)

"Dedicated to the One I Love" The Mamas and the Papas (1967)

"(Sittin' On) The Dock of the Bay" Otis Redding (1968)

"What a Wonderful World" Louis Armstrong (1968)

"El Condor Pasa (If I Could)" Simon and Garfunkel (1970)

We Can Work It Out

Dealing with Your Adult Child

THE TODDLER WHO DISPLAYED HER MAGIC MARKER TALENTS by using the living room wall as a canvas, the grade schooler who ripped her Cabbage Patch Doll during a temper tantrum, the teenybopper who went hysterical over Duran Duran, the sophomore who failed to adequately explain the dent on your new car has finally grown up to become a parent herself.

Seeing her tenderly cradle her infant, you can't help but wonder how this former tongue-pierced, back-talking, purple-haired alien will act as a loving, responsible mother. She's an adult now, which means she gets to call the shots concerning the care of her children. Still, it's difficult for you to stop parenting, just like it is for most of us.

We boomers have spent the last couple of decades telling our children to clean their rooms, brush their teeth, take driver's ed, get their degrees. Even though they're grown, it's only natural for us to keep right on telling them what to do. We speak from years of experience. Unfortunately, the new parents generally are not in the mood to listen.

We rationalize by claiming all we want is the best possible care for our grandchildren and, besides, the parents are so new at their job. But the reality is that they are grown up and in charge of their lives, family, and future. Whether we like it or not, they have their own way of doing things, which may go counter to our way of parenting. They get to choose their own style and make their own mistakes; they no longer are bound by our parenting beliefs and rules.

However, even though we know we must let go of the reins to our adult children, they are still our *children*. Forever. It doesn't matter how old any of us are.

Allan: *"Here I was a grandfather, yet my dad was still trying to tell me how to parent. For example, we were on a family outing on a brisk day, and he urged me to convince my daughter to put a jacket on her son. My dad got upset with me when I refused."*

The Don't Ask, Don't Tell Dilemma

Should you offer the new parents unsolicited advice if you honestly believe it's for the good of your grandchild, or should you do a Clarabelle and never say a word? Most experts believe you should clam up, but there is some wiggle room on this issue.

In most situations, suggests Dr. T. Berry Brazelton, you should bite your tongue. "When we see our children begin to act as parents, we get a little jealous—and competitive—and wish that they would do things our way," he explains. "But you can't tell your child, 'Do things my way.' That's very destructive to anybody's self-image. And competition like that undermines the grandchildren."

However, the noted pediatrician thinks that we boomers may have a tough time keeping our lips sealed. "Your generation was particularly narcissistic and you thought you knew everything." (You mean we *don't*?)

Margery Facklam in *Grandparents Today*: *"We wouldn't be rude enough to tell a friend how to feed her baby or how we feel about pacifiers. But we throw manners to the wind to impose our opinions on our children. We don't seem to think it strange to ask complex tax advice from an accountant-daughter and then tell her the next minute, 'You're starving this baby. When are you going to start giving him cereal?'"*

Dad on the Net: *"My parents give my wife and me a great deal of advice on how to discipline our kids, how to educate them, and even how to change diapers. But some of their advice is so outdated . . . they don't realize times have changed, kids have changed, and some of the old discipline techniques have changed for a reason. I want my parents to be involved, but right now* *they're too involved. But I don't want to put them off by saying anything for fear that they'll become less involved."*

"If you give your adult children unsolicited advice or suggestions, you have to be aware that you are undercutting them," says Dr. Brazelton. "They are liable to take it as criticism, no matter how well meant the advice is. It is wise for any grandparent to sit back and shut up and wait until the adult child turns to you. Otherwise, it can be destructive in most cases."

Such unsolicited advice often adds to the strain of an already stressed-out family, he said. Today's parents are overloaded with volumes of material on parenting. "The backlash of all the knowledge we have about child development and parenting is that parents today feel, 'Oh, gosh, everybody knows how to parent but me.' That puts them in a bind and [unwanted advice] only increases the stress, transmitting an even more stressful environment to the children."

Sue (Nana) Crawford: *"Chrisy will call me for advice but when I give her advice, she doesn't want to hear it. Chrisy has read and read and read [parenting books] and I think she depends on them too much. With our generation, we went on instinct. We probably knew much less then than our [adult] children do now, but I think we did a decent job. I think young mothers almost have too much information."*

Ray (Papa) Villwock: *"When it comes to advice, they don't ask and I don't tell."*

"Grandparents can do much harm if they're not careful and aren't respectful of what their children are trying to do," says Dr. Brazelton. "Learning to parent is learning from mistakes, not from successes. Maybe the best thing a grandparent can do is watch the parents make mistakes, then be ready to help them when they realize they've made a boo-boo.

"Remember that your job as a grandparent is to be supportive. If you really think that things need to be changed, sit down with your children and try to understand the reasons for the way they deal with their children."

> **Dad on the Net:** *"I love my parents and want them to be a big part of our kids' lives. But I want them to respect our rules even when we're not there. My parents live nearby, so they see us often. They live on a lake, and we want the children [nonswimming toddlers] to wear PFDs [personal floatation devices] while out on the dock. My parents are offended if I mention this to them . . . 'We wouldn't let anything happen to them!' Same fight about car seats . . . 'We're careful drivers—never had an accident!' I think my mom thinks we just sit around making up weird rules so that we are 'in control' of their relationships with the kids. Yes, we've tried explaining, to seemingly deaf ears, or at best, scorn for our position. And, after all, this is a control issue."*

> **Sandi (Grammy) Kingman:** *"I think my daughter is super cautious about safety concerning my two grandkids. However, I respect her wishes as a parent because it eases her mind when she leaves the kids with me."*

Dr. Perry Buffington sees nothing wrong in offering advice—if done in a loving, respectful manner. "It's difficult keeping your mouth shut when your adult children do something you don't like," he says. "This is a common problem, especially among boomers who are used to speaking up. However, there are ways to point out concerns to your children without being argumentative. If you say, 'Why in heaven's name are you doing that?' the 'why' word will create such a defensiveness like hell hath no fury.

"Here's how to deal with it: Ask questions, but in a way that doesn't trigger defensiveness from the parents. Basically, you're searching for more information. For example, 'Could you tell me more about this parenting technique you learned? Or, 'Will you explain this to me so I can understand it?' Take the word 'why' out of the question. In a medical situation in which you aren't comfortable with the parents' answers, perhaps you could ask, 'Have you considered getting a second opinion?' Maybe, if you are in a position to do so, you could follow up your question with, 'I'll pay for it.'"

If you're still not satisfied with the parents' responses, Dr. Buffington says you can show your concern without making it look like interference by stating your case. "You say, 'I am concerned about this and here is why.' And then look for the remedy." Don't push, he warns, because it will raise your child's hackles. "Remember, the parent has the final say. If you as a grandparent try to control everything, you are doomed to fail."

Adds Dr. Arthur Kornhaber, "You're a parent and a grandparent. Your children and their children look up to you as the head and the heart of the family. As a grandparent, you have the responsibility to build the family and the family continuum, the family ego, the family philosophy, the family values. That's important. Don't meddle but certainly care and give advice. All through history, grandparents were the teachers, and it doesn't stop now. You have lived longer than the kids. You know more."

> **Boomer G-Ma:** *"I voice my way of doing what I think is right. I guess even if they [her adult children] don't agree, it can't be that bad because they keep coming back for more. Aw, hell, they think I'm nuts and probably go along with me just to pacify me. Boy, have I got one over on them."*

When dealing with the way Allison and Dan are raising our grandsons Chad and Danny, we pretty much repeat to ourselves the mantra "keep quiet." Sure, we'd do some things differently. But it doesn't matter. Chad and Danny are our grandsons, not our sons. We are not in charge of them, their parents, or their parenting. The moments we became grandparents, our relationship with Allison and Dan evolved to a different level.

Like every grandparent, we've had to learn diplomacy, tact, and a sensitivity to how our words and actions could affect our relationship with the parents. Whenever we get the urge to tell them what to do, we simply think back to when we were new parents and how we felt when our parents tried to give us unsolicited advice. We hated it!

When Allison and Dan ask for our advice, we give our opinion and then leave it up to them (and suffer in silence when they decide our advice sucks).

Allan: *"One of the biggest kicks I've had as a grandparent is watching Allison turn into a terrific mother. It's a real joy for me. She and Dan are doing such a great job that I seldom have the urge to offer suggestions on how to parent."*

We tend to agree with Dr. Lillian Carson, who wrote in her book *The Essential Grandparent:* "Don't kid yourself by thinking that asking a question isn't really interference. I've done it myself only to realize later that I was not only expressing my concern but suggesting what I'd like them to do. Although it is more tactful to ask, 'Do you think you should call the doctor?' it is still a judgment. Even your tone of voice conveys a message. We must earn the right to voice our opinion by establishing a supportive relationship with praise, encouragement and assistance."

Jane (Grandmom) Whitfield: *"Do I ever see them [her adult children] make what I think is a mistake? Yes, but I keep my mouth shut. I know they are perfectly capable and they'll figure it out."*

Kathryn: *"As I was about to change Chad's diaper for the first time, I paused to admire my tiny newborn grandson. Mistaking my dawdling for hesitancy, my son-in-law Dan said, 'Let me show you how to do it.' I laughed inside. Here was this new father, who hadn't changed a diaper in his life until his son was born, telling me, a woman who has changed a million of them, how to do it. I let him show me. I enjoyed seeing the sense of accomplishment on his face after he put a diaper and sleeper on Chad and handed him to me. After Dan left the room, I turned Chad's jammies around. For some reason, fathers tend to put baby clothes on backward. I'll always remember the warm glow in Dan's eyes. I saw that same look in Allan's eyes the first time he changed Allison. And, yes, he put her clothes on backward too."*

Although most experts agree it's wise to express your opinions as infrequently as possible when it comes to the parenting of your grand-child, there are times when you absolutely need to voice your concern. If you are convinced that what the parent is doing has potential to harm the child emotionally or physically, you have an obligation to speak up.

"I believe that, while grandparents should not be intrusive, they should be forthcoming in identifying critical issues and be willing to help in difficult times," says Dr. Kornhaber. His Grandparent Study identified many grandparents who stepped in during troubled times to save children from drug-addicted or abusive parents.

The Family Hour

How well your advice is received often depends on how well you give it. "I believe in family conferences," says Dr. Kornhaber. "If I want to tell my son-in-law or daughter something, I'll take one of them out to lunch. I'm not going to say, 'You're a jerk for doing this.' I'm going to put it in a very loving, noncritical, and supportive way.

"People should sit down and lovingly let their feelings out and tell each other how they feel. I'll always give my opinion in a nice way— and I'm willing to accept my children's opinion. It's a two-way street. I don't think giving advice is meddling and controlling."

> **Tom (Grandpa) Andersen:** *"I read somewhere that when it comes to communicating between grandparents and their adult children, follow the example of your newborn grandchild: Let people know how you feel, rest, and spend lots of time listening."*

"Issues should be discussed," says Dr. Kornhaber. "Grandchildren have to understand that Mom and Dad and Grandma and Grandpa don't have to agree on everything, that conflict is normal, that prob-lems are normal, that emotions are normal. You might have a fight, but if you're committed to each other, you come out the other end okay. It's great modeling for kids."

Here are some tips from experts on how to hold a family conference with your adult children:

- If you take the lead in opening the discussion, choose a time
  when nobody is tired or angry.
- Stick to one issue. Don't try to discuss a laundry list of problems.
- State your feelings or concerns as clearly as possible without
  attacking the parents.
- Find ways to compromise.
- Remain calm and treat each other with mutual respect.
- Don't belittle or undermine the confidence of the new parents.
  Instead, provide encouragement and sympathy.

"Allow everyone to express their feelings and point of view," says
Dr. Kornhaber. "Indirect and roundabout communication gets nothing
done. All it does is foment anger, frustration, and disappointment. Be
direct and open with your feelings. Then come to an acceptable
understanding. Usually everyone's love for the children involved can
bring folks together."

Being blunt is a boomer trait. Adds Dr. Buffington, "Grandparents
have more experience and they know that their lives are more than
half over, so they tend to be more direct and understanding, especially
boomers."

Psychologist and boomer grandmother Dr. Anya Luchow Liberman
says it's important to engage in family discussions even if you don't
have high expectations of getting problems resolved. "I encourage
open sharing. You have to accept people for who they are and not pro-
ject your needs onto them. It's important to validate the other person's
feelings. For example, 'I hear what you're saying and I understand
where you're coming from, but you might not be aware of my thoughts
on this.' Then let it go. Share your feelings, disappointments, and
expectations. Beyond that, above all else, you must recognize your
adult children's right to make whatever decision they make.

"Unless you see something that smacks of potential danger, you
should keep your mouth shut when it comes to unasked advice.
Accept the fact that the parents have a right to do it their way even if

it's different than the way you did it. You need to remind yourself that you didn't always listen to your parents."

When her daughter's doctor wanted to induce labor, nana-to-be Pat Connolly asked pointed questions that left the doctor irritated and her daughter confused. Here, with her permission, is what the cyber-columnist wrote about the experience:

> An awkward situation was developing here and I definitely had something to say. But how do I say it? Or do I even say it? My son-in-law was very committed to the doctor's viewpoint. My daughter wasn't sure. And I thought more questions needed to be asked.
>
> I recognized a dilemma that would come up again and again in life surrounding important decisions with my grown children. How much do I say? What was my motive? Was it to give them my viewpoint from years of experience or to make sure that they handled the situation my way? I could try to get them to do what I thought was right (as I had when they were children) or I could step back and let go of this phase of the parent-child relationship.
>
> When we parents complained that our children didn't appear to grow up or make the right decisions, maybe there was something else going on that we failed to see. Maybe we continued to decide what they should or shouldn't do—and we let them know in subtle or not so subtle ways.
>
> When I examined my point of view, I saw that this part of my job as a parent was done. Just as I would do for any friend, my job now was to tell my daughter and son-in-law what I thought, then step back and let them make their decision. It was time to let them know that I'll be there, but I won't interfere.
>
> Not to impulsively act as a parent was very difficult. It was a new way of thinking for me. After all those years of raising them, I no longer had the final word. If I had continued in the old direction, there would be no growing in our relationship as adults. There might not even be a relationship, because most adults resent others interfering in their lives.

I sat down with my daughter and her husband and told them my thoughts and anxieties on inducing labor. Then I said, "I'll support whatever you decide." They decided to follow the doctor's advice. What could have been a disaster in our relationship was averted. I understand now that I can make life easier for my adult children and me if I can distinguish when I'm being the parent and when I'm being a friend.

Involvement Versus Interfering

"A lot of grandparents pussyfoot around because they're afraid of meddling," says Dr. Kornhaber. "They try to be very sophisticated and not pushy, but they end up not making their wishes and needs known to the parents." As a result, he adds, sometimes parents don't involve grandparents on the wrong assumption that the grandparents aren't interested in the family.

"Speak up. One of the problems is that there are too many elders and too many adult children who wrongly think grandparents' interest means meddling and advice means controlling. I hate that. Offering advice in a noncritical way and showing interest in the grandchildren means you're loving and supportive. Parents can always refuse the grandparents' advice.

"On the other hand, I hear parents say the grandparents don't care. The parents never offer to explain their needs. They don't want to ask Mom and Dad to baby-sit because they feel sorry for the grandparents. This kind of stuff stifles open communication."

Jane (Grandmom) Whitfield: *"As the mother of married sons, I feel somewhat left out. While I communicate with the boys, men do not communicate to the extent women do. Men don't go into detail, and I love the details."*

Nana Pat: *"I offer advice more to my son than to my daughter-in-law. I'll say to him, 'Now whatever you do, don't say anything* *to her' because there's nothing worse than, 'My mom says this and that.'"*

As a grandparent, you never know how your comments will be received. When you think you are helping your children with sound suggestions, they may think you're meddling. If you don't offer advice, your children may think you don't care. So what do you do?

Suggests Dr. Buffington: "One of the best ways to avoid interfering when you want to help is to simply say, 'I want to do more but I'm afraid of meddling.' Honesty is always in order. Be adult. Don't play games. If you want to do or know something, ask. But be prepared for an answer that you don't want to hear.

"Usually, though, parents are often so overwhelmed they are looking for someone to help them. So if you happen to be standing there, make it known you're available. You'll get the chance to help out and improve your relationship with your adult child. Be there and show an interest in helping care for your grandchild."

Sue (Nana) Crawford: *"I told [her daughter] Chrisy that I wouldn't baby-sit full-time. But I meet her and the kids [a toddler and an infant] and do things together. She and I also share a job working for my husband. I keep the kids when she works. It seems to help Chrisy to get out of the house."*

The parent-grandparent relationship often affects, and is affected by, the level of involvement in the family by the grandparent.

"When grandparents are involved with grandchildren, it really helps marriages," says Dr. Kornhaber. "It takes a lot of the pressure off because the parents may be able to go off alone for a weekend or a vacation. It shows that the grandparents are still loving parents."

Nana on the Net: *"My husband's parents live only twenty minutes away. It seems that we only see them for special occasions, and although we have invited them over and occasionally asked for baby-sitting help, they never seem to have the time. Okay, but I*

*don't want to hear any whining that 'My grandchildren don't
know me.'"*

According to the Grandparent Study, not only were the parents
missing their parents' involvement, but the grandchildren were too.
Reports Dr. Kornhaber: "One young mother sadly complained that her
own father lived two blocks away yet never took the time to spend
more than an occasional hour with her children. When I spoke with
this grandfather, he said that he didn't want to 'meddle' in his daughter's life. He thought that he was doing his daughter a favor by allowing her to be 'independent.'

"One of the most frequent reasons for grandparent-parent non-
involvement is lack of communication. Many parents are hesitant about
asking their parents to be more involved because they feel guilty
about doing so. A young father told me, 'My parents have worked hard all
of their lives. I don't have the right to ask them to get involved in
mine.' The truth is, however, that young parents do have a right to at
least ask their own parents for time and attention. Parents are parents
for the rest of their lives.

"Some grandparents don't want to become involved even if they are
asked. As one uninvolved grandmother said, 'I raised my kids and now I
want time for myself.' Her son thought she was very selfish and self-
centered. Under these circumstances the only thing an 'abandoned'
parent can do is to involve a third party—a friend, a clergyperson, a
therapist—to sit down with the family."

Playing by the Rules

Barbara Bowman, president of the Erikson Institute, believes it's coun-
terproductive to keep silent if the rules for the grandchildren in your
house are different than those at your adult child's. "If you're sweating
under the collar and it just makes you furious, then it's crazy to keep
your mouth shut," she says. "You need to sit down and communicate in
an honest, tactful way. Families work best when people have mutual
respect and can find solutions together.

"My daughter and I agreed that when my granddaughter is at my house, she obeys my rules. For instance, at her home she can put her feet on the table. When she's at my house, her feet go under the table. She quickly learned what she can do at home and at her grandmother's. There are things she can do at my house that she can't do at home. I give her much more freedom when playing by herself. But I'm more a stickler for manners."

Alisa (Nana) Dollar: *"I don't agree with [the discipline method] 'time out,' but I adhere to the method when I keep the grandchildren. I have them for such a short time, so I follow the rules."*

Papa on the Net: *"The parents let them [his grandchildren, ages two and four] run wild at home, but I don't in my house. I have no problem setting rules when they come over. They might as well learn now that their behavior at home isn't necessarily going to be tolerated elsewhere, like when they start school."*

Dr. Brazelton suggests that you exercise some restraint when disciplining the grandkids. "You don't want to endanger what your own children are doing with their children. Don't get into it, but if you must, you'd better have thought out how you want to handle discipline. If you're impulsive and overreact, you'll lose respect and might do something you don't believe in."

To build trust with your adult child, you need to play by his or her rules—most of the time, says Dr. Buffington. "If the parent says, 'I don't let my child have cookies,' don't give him cookies. However, every once in a while you should violate the rule just a little bit and whisper, 'Don't tell your mother.' It's like a secret bonding that every child remembers with his grandparents. You want that to happen occasionally. The truth is the parent wants you to do that too."

On the other hand, make sure you understand the reason why the parents don't want your grandson to have peanut butter cookies. He might be deathly allergic to them.

Doing It Again—Only Better

Occasionally we grandparents might lash out at a behavior that we helped cause, says Dr. Buffington. "Sometimes the parents don't know any other way to behave. When you see the adult child behave this way, you think, 'Oh, God, that's the way I taught him.' You see yourself—and that can be very painful.

"Sometimes when I counsel young parents, they say, 'I don't want suggestions from my parents or in-laws on parenting.' I reply, 'Get a grip. Your wish will never happen.' You never miss the water till the well runs dry. What the parents are really saying is 'I don't want the grandparents controlling my kid.' That's what they're most afraid of."

Because of painful memories of their own childhood, some parents are reluctant to let the grandparents too close to the grandkids, says Dr. Kornhaber. "During counseling sessions, I've had parents say, 'Well, my parents screwed me up during my childhood, so they'll screw up my kids.' I reply, 'No they won't, because now they know they screwed you up and they aren't going to let that happen again.'"

Boomers' children—members of Generation X—are the first of the new era of divorce to reach adulthood. Between 1970 and 1990, the number of children living with only their mothers doubled, from 11 percent to 22 percent, according to census figures.

William Strauss, author of *Generations*, cites childhood divorce as one of the decisive experiences influencing how Gen Xers shape their own families. Above all, they want to avoid creating the broken homes, alimony disputes, absentee fathers, and tangles with stepparents that many of them experienced as children, he says. In many cases, this upbringing affects the way Gen Xers deal with their parents now that the Gen Xers are having children of their own. They don't want to create the same kind of broken homes that they grew up in.

But, according to the Grandparent Study, in their relationships with their grandchildren, 68 percent of the grandparents reported they tended not to repeat the same mistakes they had made with their own children. "It was as if they learned from their experience and nature gave them another chance," says Dr. Kornhaber. In the study, a majority of adult children felt the grandparents had displayed much better parenting skills now than when they were parents.

Many young dads are surprised to see their once-domineering, punitive fathers become old softies around their grandchildren. Erik Erikson wrote that grandparenting was an opportunity for men to make peace with their child-rearing pasts. In an Australian study, grandfathers reported enjoying their grandchildren more than their own sons and saw their involvement as a way to make up for lost opportunities with their own children. The benefits may span generations: By watching their once-distant fathers with their grandchildren, men may vicariously enjoy what they themselves missed years before, and relieve some of their lingering resentment.

You might actually get gently chided by the parents for being such a doting grandparent. "If your adult daughter or son says, 'You were never that nice to me,' don't resent it," says Dr. Brazelton. "They are recognizing that you have learned something since they were kids. Graciously acknowledge you have learned a thing or two in your time."

Staying Tight with the Gatekeepers

Your relationship with your adult child can have a profound affect—good or bad—on your grandchild.

"It's real simple," says Dr. Buffington. "Because the parents technically control access to the grandchild and are the gatekeepers, it's important for you to develop a good relationship with the gatekeepers."

If you're on excellent terms with your adult child, it's likely you'll have a good relationship with your grandchild. However, says Dr. Kornhaber, "even if you have a bad relationship with your adult child, you can still have a good one with your grandchild—if you spend time alone with him. But if Mom is there and you aren't getting along with her, the poor kid gets the fallout."

The experts agree that you should never talk to your grandchild in a negative way about his parents. It won't help him and could only make matters worse for you.

"The adults all have to love the kid more than they bug each other," says Dr. Kornhaber. "The parents are the linchpin of the relationship and really control a lot of it. But if you just leave the grandparent and the grandchild alone, for the most part it's wonderful. If the parents don't get along with the grandparents, the parents have to understand that it has nothing to do with the relationship between the grandparent and the grandchild.

"Every family should find ways for the grandparent to spend time alone with the grandchild because that relationship is a separate human connection. The best thing parents can do is to get out of the way and tell the kid to go off with Grandma and Grandpa and have a good time."

The Other Grandparents

Grandchildren are meant to be shared.

In the ideal situation, both sets (or, in some cases, multiple sets) of grandparents are respectful of each other and allow their grandchildren to have a thriving relationship with each of them without any jealousy. The children feel loved and so do their elders. Everybody wins.

However, grandparents who don't get along with each other or compete to be the No. 1 nana or papa can create upheaval in the family and, ultimately, harm the very relationships they are striving so hard to achieve with their grandchildren. Conflicts between maternal and paternal grandparents are often triggered by intolerance to one another's culture, religion, race, or socioeconomic status as well as differences in personal values, politics, and lifestyles. Then again, maybe it's simply bad chemistry.

"When a grandparent attempts to fill a grandchild's mind with propaganda about having a special or exclusionary relationship, it not only hurts the child, but it also alienates the other grandparents," says Dr. Kornhaber. "Children abhor demands for loyalty and choosing one adult over another."

> **Long-distance grandmom:** *"My husband and I don't get along with the other grandparents. They're obnoxious, aggressive, and very wealthy. They buy our grandson all sorts of expensive toys. They even set up a train in their living room that he can ride.*

They're trying to buy his love. We can't afford to do that. There's no sense talking to the parents because they aren't very assertive. So all we can do is try to make every moment with him a fun, interesting, and memorable time that he will cherish as much as we do."

"It's the experience grandkids remember more than the package they unwrap," says Dr. Buffington. "In a child's life, attention has more value than things. Loving that child and being there for him plays a greater part in that child's memory than do material things."

Rather than get into a competition of which set of grandparents can shower the grandkids with the most presents or the most expensive ones, many parents choose to limit the number and/or the cost of individual gifts from the grandparents.

"Parents have enough to deal with without having to straighten out problems between grandparents who should know better," says Dr. Kornhaber. "When conflicts arise, grandparents should take the lead in resolving them. After all, grandparents are supposed to set a good example for the rest of the family."

> **Frustrated mom:** *"There's so much jealousy between the two sets of grandparents. I have to make sure that if my kids do something with one set, then, by God, I better grant the other set the same amount of time with them or there is hell to pay."*

In our own situation, we (and, for that matter, our grandsons) feel blessed that Chad's and Danny's paternal grandparents, Trent and Mary Lou Manausa, live fifteen minutes away from them in Tallahassee, because we live five hundred miles away. We four grandparents each have something distinctive to offer the boys in our own style, personality, passions, and activities, so there is no need for competition or feelings of jealousy. Papa Manausa and Mama Lou have their own special rituals, traditions, and pastimes with the boys that are different than the ones we have with the kids. For example, the grandsons go fishing with Papa Manausa, have their exclusive lunch-and-a-movie with Mama

Lou, go hiking with Papa Zullo, and make pasta by hand with Nana.

We're happy that the kids get to see their paternal grandparents regularly so they can nurture their relationship. When we visit Tallahassee, our days center solely around Chad and Danny. The Manausas are so understanding that they let us hog the time with the boys. However, during holidays and special events, the entire extended family gets together for a wonderful time.

We honor, respect, and genuinely like each other. Besides, we all share a common goal—to make our grandchildren feel loved.

Bridge Over Troubled Water

Dealing with Blended and Nontraditional Families

WHEN WE BOOMERS WERE GROWING UP, Ozzie and Harriet typified the American family. Dad was the sole breadwinner (forget the fact that Ozzie never seemed to work) and Mom stayed home with the kids. Divorce was almost unheard of.

Today, children are just as likely to live with a single parent, grandparents, stepparents, or nonrelatives as they are to live in the traditional nuclear family. It's not surprising when you look at the following statistics gleaned from the U.S. Census Bureau and the Stepfamily Foundation:

- 1,300 new stepfamilies are formed every day.
- 66 percent of all marriages and living-together situations involving children end in breakup.
- 50 percent of children will be victims of a divorce before they are eighteen.
- 50 percent of the children under the age of thirteen are living with one biological parent and that parent's partner.

Now some boomer grandparents are asking such questions as, "What do our former daughter-in-law's children from her new marriage call us?" "Can we take our grandchildren to the ballgame without upsetting their stepsiblings?" "Is it okay to feel jealous of our grandson's affection for his stepgrandmother?"

If Your Adult Child Divorces

Divorce has profound repercussions for all family members. Each year, one million children suffer through the split-up of their parents.

Dr. Arthur Kornhaber calls grandparents the "other victims of divorce" because their relationship with their grandchildren can be severely compromised. "Parental divorce can affect grandparents' time with grandchildren, for better or worse," he says. "Helping and supporting the custodial mother may increase the time that grandparents spend with their grandchildren. However, if parents remarry or another set of grandparents takes on a supportive role, grandparents' time with, and access to, their grandchildren may be compromised.

"Parental divorce affects grandparents adversely, especially when they are helpless to do anything about the situation. The matter is complicated even further when grandparents are enmeshed in the divorced couple's problems or when they are emotionally attached to their children's ex-spouse."

Family psychologist Dr. Anya Luchow Liberman says when there is a divorce with children involved, she often urges the grandparents not to cut off ties with the former spouse of their adult child. "I think it's really important to the grandkids to realize that a divorce doesn't necessarily mean everything gets cut in half. They can still see Daddy's mother even though they're living with Mommy. Grandparents tend to take sides, but for the kids, it's so much nicer if there's an ongoing relationship with the former spouse—even if it's somewhat superficial. You do it for the sake of the grandkids.

"I speak from a personal point of view. When I was married to my children's father, I had the absolutely best relationship with my in-laws. I loved my mother-in-law. During the divorce, she sat down with her son and said, 'I'm not choosing sides. I love you. You are always my son. But I love Anya too and she is my grandchildren's mother.' She maintained a wonderful, close relationship with me until the day she died. It was wonderful for my kids, who were two and five when we divorced. They loved the fact that Nana could come to visit them at Mommy's house. She made time for her son and time for me. I loved it; it wasn't awkward. She was a great role model for unconditional love. It makes such a difference for the children."

According to the nonprofit research firm Child Trends, studies indicate that those grandparents whose adult child does not have legal custody of the children have a decreased amount of contact with their grandchildren, especially if they don't live nearby. The same studies show that proximity to the children's custodial parent is a major factor in maintaining a continued grandparent-grandchild relationship. Grandchildren of divorced, single-parent families report higher levels of closeness with the parents of the custodial parent and are more likely to turn to them for support than are grandchildren of two-parent families. In times of family distress, such as divorce, grandparents report extending higher levels of emotional support as well as parent-like behavior toward their grandchildren.

Dr. Kornhaber says the quality of the relationship of grandparents to the surviving custodial parent (whether or not they are blood related) can determine the degree of grandparent access to the grandchildren. Even if the relationship is less than desired, you can take steps to protect your right to visit your grandchild after the divorce. (See the chapter on legal issues.)

If your adult child divorces, you probably will experience some of the same feelings as your grandchild—helplessness over events beyond your control, anger over the situation, anxiety about the future, and sadness over a broken family. Unfortunately, you both must suffer the consequences of the split-up.

"It's virtually impossible not to take sides when your child is getting a divorce," says Dr. Perry Buffington. "The body is not wired to be neutral in these circumstances. The key point is how much anger, piss, and vinegar do you spew as the result of taking a side. As long as you're not yelling, screaming, or swearing and you're being straightforward, that minimizes the damage to your grandchild during and after divorce. Try to keep things as factual and emotionally objective as you can.

"You need to remember that whatever problems your grandchild had before the divorce will be intensified after the divorce. The best adjusted children after a divorce are those who saw the least amount of anger from the grandparents and the sparring parents."

Some tips from the experts:

- Focus your attention on your grandchild, not on the parents. During this time of turmoil, she needs your love, support, and understanding more than anyone.

- Be aware that your grandchild may believe she is responsible for the breakup, a feeling that often leads to a poor self-image. Reassure her that she is not the cause, that it's an adult problem that adults must solve.
- Praise her whenever possible and build up her self-esteem. Do your best not to criticize her during this difficult time.
- Encourage her to express her feelings. Give her the opportunity to open up and share her concerns and fears. If you have more than one grandchild in the household, spend time with each one separately so they can talk to you in private.
- Be someone she can count on. Phone or visit regularly no matter what. Be consistent so she knows you will always be there for her.
- Fight the urge to take sides. Your grandchild has only one biological mother and one biological father, so avoid doing or saying something that could hurt her relationship with either parent.
- Be honest with your grandchild, but that doesn't mean you must reveal any or all of the sordid details.
- Remind her repeatedly that she is loved by you and her parents. Tell her that even if her parents are angry at each other, they still love her and that she doesn't have to stop loving one parent to show affection toward the other.
- Ask her and your adult child how you can help. If they tell you, follow through.
- Find ways to create positive, fun experiences for your grandchild.
- Ask the divorcing parents to make provisions in their divorce agreement for your right to see your grandchild.
- Do all you can to help your grandchild adjust if a parent begins dating or remarries.

This is the time when your grandchild needs you more than ever, says Barbara Bowman, president of the Erikson Institute. "If you want to have contact with your grandchildren when they grow up, you better be with them when they're young. Swallow your pride if you must.

Talk to the parents about how important it is for you not to lose touch with the grandchildren. Even if everyone is furious with one another, the goal is to prevent the children from experiencing harm."

If You Divorce

If you are the one going through a divorce, you can still maintain a close relationship with your grandchild and ease her pain.

"I think this situation involves the same kind of issues as when the parents divorce but to a much lesser extent," says family expert Dr. Gregory Sanders. "The child is not going to be as torn or caught in the middle. Both grandparents need to tell her that their closeness to her won't change, but that some things about the relationship will change, if only slightly. For example, 'You won't come to Grandma and Grandpa's house, but you will see us at our own separate places. We'll keep doing things with you; they just won't be with Grandma and Grandpa together. We may not both be there for holidays but we will continue to have special times with you.' Her parents can play a role too by encouraging a closeness in the relationship."

However, the grandparents' breakup can have an adverse affect on the adult children, threatening the stability of the family. "Things will never be the same, but it's up to you to try to keep your relationship with your children and grandchildren as consistent as possible," says Dr. Buffington. "You need to reassure your grandchild that you'll still be there for her. Do it not only with your words but with your actions. That means you should continue to do the things you used to do with her before the divorce.

"It's not unusual for a divorced grandparent to latch onto their adult children for support. You're looking for validation that you did the right thing. It's only human to do that. But be careful about dumping all your troubles on them and try not to criticize your spouse in front of the family." He also warns of the difficult position you could put your adult children in if you refuse to attend a family function solely because your ex-spouse will be there.

Dr. Liberman says she tells divorcing couples: "Don't lose sight of the fact that there was a time in your life when you wanted to spend your whole life together. After you get divorced, try to hold on to a little piece of that memory of how much you loved that person." She reminds divorcing grandparents to keep that memory in mind when they are talking about their former spouses to their grandchildren and adult children.

Grandfathers are especially impacted by divorce, says Dr. Valarie King, assistant professor of sociology, demography and human development and family studies at Penn State University. In her 2002 study, she found that divorced grandfathers report much less contact, fewer shared activities, and higher levels of conflict with their grandchildren than divorced grandmothers and never-divorced grandparents.

Dr. King also found that the detrimental impact of divorce on grandparent-grandchild relationships is greater for paternal grandparents than it is for maternal grandparents. However, she adds, a good parent-grandparent relationship can ease the negative influence of a grandparent's divorce on the relationship between grandparent and grandchild.

Not all aspects of grandparenting are affected by divorce, she says. Divorced grandparents are just as likely as married grandparents to discuss their grandchild's future, share skills, or act as mentors to their grandchildren. Additionally, grandparents who have divorced are more likely to discuss problems with their grandchildren.

Some tips from the experts:

- Understand that your divorce has severe repercussions for all family members, especially grandchildren.

- Let family members know the facts of the divorce and listen to their thoughts and feelings.

- Respect the grieving process of all family members, especially the grandchildren who might feel disappointment, disorientation, and insecurity.

- Be respectful of, and do not interfere with, family members' relationship with the divorced spouse.

- If your grandchild asks specific questions, answer frankly, according to her age and need to know.

If You Become a Stepgrandparent

A recent study noted that one-third of grandparents interviewed had at least one stepgrandchild. While most grandparents acquire stepgrandchildren when an adult child remarries, other nanas and papas gain stepgrandkids after remarrying following a divorce or a spouse's death. For a child, the remarriage of each of her parents can potentially add four stepgrandparents. And, in that same scenario, if the biological grandparents divorce and remarry . . . well, you get the picture.

Dr. Sanders, of the Department of Child Development and Family Science at North Dakota State University, conducted one of the first studies ever on stepgrandparents. Contrary to the image of the wicked stepfamily, he and researcher Debra Trygstad found some encouraging news for stepgrandparents. In over half the cases, the stepgrandchildren (who were college students at the time of the study) regarded their stepgrandparents in a positive way.

"Most of the stepgrandchildren in this study viewed the stepgrandparent not only as someone they cared for as an individual, but also as someone they respected," says Dr. Sanders. The study found that stepgrandchildren maintain contact with their stepgrandparents beyond high school; the majority of respondents wanted more contact with their stepgrandparents; and almost half the respondents viewed their relationship with their stepgrandparents as important.

"The stepgrandchildren wanted to see their stepgrandparents more than they had the opportunity to," Dr. Sanders reports. "It's very good that older people can become involved in children's lives and have a positive impact and a positive relationship even without a biological bond."

The Sanders-Trygstad study asked the respondents to answer questions concerning the one stepgrandparent that they saw most often. Among the results:

- 89 percent of the respondents believed that the stepgrandparent deserved respect.
- 67 percent believed they could learn a lot from their stepgrandparent.

- 50 percent said having a personal relationship with their step-grandparent was very important.

- 46 percent described their emotional attachment to their step-grandparent as pleasurable.

"Although not a majority, many saw the relationship as important or extremely important," says Dr. Sanders. "These findings indicate that the relationship goes beyond a formal tie and involves actual interaction and meaning to the family system.

"New stepfamilies might begin to understand the importance of establishing relationships with stepgrandparents, especially when the children are young. The relationship with their stepgrandparents has potential for becoming an additional resource to their family. Children who have stepgrandparents may have an extra set of relatives they can turn to for support."

If you are a stepgrandparent, realize that children don't require a genetic link in order for them to love you and develop a good relationship with you. Children respond to adults who shower them with affection, attention, and nurturing.

> **Stepgrandparent Diane Marquette:** *"Even if you are one of three or more grandmothers or grandfathers in a child's life, don't concern yourself about competing with the 'natural' grandparents. This is not a contest. There is enough love to go around. As my mother-in-law told me when my older stepgrandson was born: 'They bring their own love with them.' So, yes, there is enough love to go around."*

Dr. Sanders says there are several factors that will determine how easy it will be to develop your relationship with your stepgrandchild. Among the most important:

- The age of the child when you enter her life. The younger she is, the better the chances are that you will forge a close relationship. "You have more time to develop the relationship," says Dr.

Sanders. "The older she is, the less likely that you'll be important in her life."

- The child's relationship with her stepparent (your adult child).
  "If she doesn't get along with her stepparent, then the relationship with her stepgrandparent is not going to be fully developed
  or seen as important," he says. In the study, the more dissatisfied
  the child was with her parent's remarriage, the lower she rated
  the importance of the relationship with her stepgrandparents.

- Your relationship with your adult child and his or her new
  spouse. The biological parent will play a role in establishing the
  amount of contact that stepgrandparents have with the parent's
  child. "Also, what role the stepparent expects his or her parents
  to play with the child is going to have a real impact on how
  involved the grandparent can be," he says. If you have a good
  relationship with the parents, then you likely will have more
  access and encouragement to develop your own relationship
  with your grandchild.

- How often you get to see the stepgrandchild. "Distance can play
  a key factor," he adds. "If you live far away and don't see her too
  often or communicate with her, then you can't expect to
  develop much of a relationship with her."

Many children may not be quick to adjust to the demands of knowing and accepting a stepparent, stepsiblings, and stepgrandparents,
says Dr. Kornhaber. "However, our studies have shown that if stepgrandparents go gently and make themselves available, without asking
for any reward or feedback such as verbal declarations of the children's
love and respect, the majority can develop significant attachments.

"Stepgrandparents need to relate to members of the extended family
and especially the stepgrandchild's caretaker. They must consider the
child's other grandparents if they are in the picture. These family
arrangements can be fraught with emotional complications that stepgrandparents must identify and deal with if they wish to have smooth
relationships with others. When the time and circumstances are right,
most children can accept a stepgrandparent. After all, the more people

a child has to love, the better. When it works, a wonderful bond is formed for life between child and stepgrandparent. But often, it isn't easy to make it work."

He says stepgrandparents can get important clues about how to act by considering and reflecting upon the conditions that made them stepgrandparents in the first place. "For example, if the child has no living grandparents, or lacks a grandparent of the same sex as the step-grandparent, the stepgrandparent can easily fill that void in the child's heart and soul for a beloved elder. There is no competition. When this works well, it deepens the bond between the biological grandparent and his or her spouse [the stepgrandparent] because they have the love of the child in common."

> **Dr. Anya (Baba) Luchow Liberman:** *"When my stepgrandson was born, I was very careful to defer to the biological grandmother because the connection between the daughter and mother is so strong. I was more like an aunt than a grandma. I made sure that she [the biological grandmother] went first in whatever was happening. I didn't hog the baby. We never talked about it. We sort of danced the dance, but did it very smoothly."*

If the child has living grandparents, the stepgrandparent still can be an important and loving friend to the child, says Dr. Kornhaber. "But the stepgrandparent has to be sensitive—letting the youngster come to the stepgrandparent and being aware of existing [biological] grandparent-grandchild relationships and what is happening in the family. There might be jealousy, envy, and more. The effective step-grandparent must be a friend to everyone and shouldn't try to rush things. Wait in the family wings before entering a child's life.

"Many stepgrandchildren I have interviewed had to deal with pro-found psychological issues such as dealing with divided loyalties, try-ing to comprehend the circumstances leading to the remarriage of the custodial parent, working through the dissolution of the parents' mar-riage, and trying to make sense of a new family configuration. This is a tall order, and the last thing a child needs is to be expected to have an instant relationship with a stepgrandparent. In fact, the child may resent a stepgrandparent at first because the child sees that person as an interloper in a once-secure family life."

Multiple sets of grandparents can make for some touchy situations, especially during holidays and special occasions. Some parents opt to alternate spending a holiday like Thanksgiving with a different set of grandparents each year, rather than trying to squeeze in multiple visits in one year.

To keep family gatherings amicable, Dr. Kornhaber recommends that parents discuss plans with the biological grandparents first and then the stepgrandparents to make sure that all the adults are on the same page. "At functions like a child's graduation, put the child's happiness first," he advises. "Above all, be gracious." The child doesn't have the same emotional baggage that the parents do, and it's up to the adults to make sure that they put their negative feelings aside for the children's sake.

Dr. Sanders says it's important for you to introduce your family traditions to your stepgrandchildren. "That will help to build the relationship and make you unique. Include your stepgrandchildren in your family history. Let them know what your rituals and traditions are because that can make you special in their eyes."

If you are a new stepgrandparent or will become one soon, don't worry about competing with the biological grandparents, says Dr. Sanders. "There really isn't a need to compete. There's room for both kinds of grandparents. The biological grandparents shouldn't feel threatened by stepgrandparents. The biological grandparents are going to continue to be the most important connection for the grandchild, but that doesn't mean the stepgrandparents can't play an important role and form a positive relationship too. Kids can't have too many people who care about them and support them."

In homes where there are stepgrandchildren as well as biological grandchildren, it can be tricky to expect the grandparent to treat everyone the same.

"It creates conflicts when kids are treated differently in the same household," Dr. Sanders says. "Differences [in how the children are treated] should be discussed openly with the grandchildren and stepgrandchildren to establish the importance of all the relationships. Being open about it will head off some bad feelings that might occur."

If you have grandkids and stepgrandkids, Dr. T. Berry Brazelton offers this simple advice: "Do the best you can. The more you can give the stepgrandchild, the better. It's a tenuous relationship at best because you are not that child's biological grandparent and you feel more committed to your own [biological] grandchildren. You can't help that. So go on and deal with it the best way you can."

Dr. Sanders suggests that you work at developing a good relationship with the parents. "The middle generation has a lot of influence over the type of relationship you'll have with your stepgrandchild. Do the parents encourage and support the relationship? What are their expectations of you? Are they willing to find ways to make this a positive experience?"

He says a fairly common concern with new stepgrandparents is what they want the stepgrandkids to call them. "Part of it depends on the age of the children at the time. It's something that needs to be worked out in the families. Calling someone 'Stepgrandpa' is quite a mouthful. I have a stepdaughter and she calls my parents by their first names. From my experience, if the children are quite young when the remarriage takes place, they might be more likely to call the step-grandparents Grandma and Grandpa."

Stepgrandparent Jane Murphy, cofounder of Grandboomers.com: *"I am lucky. I have a good relationship with my stepkids [her husband's grown daughters], and they have welcomed me into their families. When they had children, I knew not to step ahead of the biological parents or grandparents. They came to me and asked me what I would like the kids to call me. They call me Grandma Jane, and the biological grandparents are Grandma and Grandpa."*

Some tips from the experts:

- Ask the parents' permission to become involved in your step-grandchild's life.

- Seek friendship first with your stepgrandchild.
- If your biological grandchild has new stepsiblings, spend some time alone with her and offer reassurance. Listen to her fears and concerns.
- Be patient and understanding of your grandchild's feelings over her new living arrangements before you start to build a relationship with your new stepgrandkids. Children have a difficult time after a parent's death, divorce, or remarriage and are trying to make sense of their new family configuration.
- Take your time in getting to know your stepgrandchildren. If you push too hard or too fast, you risk getting rejected. Be available to those who reach out to you and stay at a loving distance to those who are negative.
- Enlist your biological grandchild into helping you develop a relationship with your stepgrandkids.
- Maintain a positive relationship with the stepgrandchildren's other grandparents and parents.

Nontraditional Families

In the days of the Cleavers, Andersons, and Stones, it was odd to have single parenthood by choice, communal living, households headed by nonparents, and same-sex relationships that included children. Today, an increasing number of boomer grandparents have adult children who are living in such nontraditional families.

Society has become more open-minded about a variety of living arrangements, family configurations, and lifestyles. As a result, according to the 2000 census report, only 24 percent of all households in America include two parents with children, 43 percent of unmarried couples include children, and 22 percent of all families with children are headed by single mothers. About 40 percent of children will live with their unmarried mother and her boyfriend some time before their sixteenth birthday, according to a study supported by the National Institute of Child Health and Human Development. While there is still some uncertainty about the number of lesbian and gay families in the United States, the marketing firm Witeck-Combs Communications estimates that between two million and three million gays are currently raising children.

"Gay and lesbian couples have adopted many children who had been literally thrown away by society," says Dr. Kornhaber. "It helps when the children have relatives in 'traditional' family arrangements too. That's why it's so important that they be welcomed into the extended family by the grandparents.

"Many new grandparents of children whose parents are gay or lesbian find that they change their attitudes and become supportive of their child's role as a parent."

If you don't approve of the family situation, don't let that interfere with your own special relationship with your grandchild, says Dr. Buffington. "Your adult child chose to be in this situation, so it's up to you to accept it.

"In some cases, I've seen grandparents not give as much love and affection to the grandchild just because they are so preoccupied about what the adult child did. The best thing to do is focus on what is in the best interests of the child." He warns that your ill feelings toward your adult child's unique family situation can weaken the bond between the parents and your grandchild.

Because of society's bias, being a part of a nontraditional family is extremely challenging. Don't add to the difficulty. "If you have trouble supporting this kind of lifestyle for your adult child and his or her child, you need to put your own prejudices aside," says Dr. Buffington. "You have a higher issue, a higher ethic to deal with—the needs of a young child. My best advice is: Grandparents, grow up! Make the child your main priority. If you don't, you are incredibly selfish. I can't think of a single, solitary, valid reason why a grandparent would not want to be around a grandchild."

If you're still having a problem dealing with your adult child's lifestyle, try seeking a professional therapist to help you work it out. Quite frankly, you should be happy that your adult child has been blessed with a child's love. The family would be even more blessed with your love and emotional support.

Interfaith, Interracial, and Intercultural Marriages

If your adult child marries someone of a different race, faith, or culture, you probably have some concerns about the way in which they plan to raise your grandchild, especially if it involves beliefs that are far different than yours.

> **Nana Lana:** *"When we all get together, it's like a mini-United Nations. Jews, Gentiles, Irish, Bahamian, French, Poles. For the holidays, we all bring something for the table. When [grandchildren] Sammy and Mandy get a little older, they will really appreciate their melting-pot heritage."*

Dr. Buffington believes you should show your grandchild who you are by the way you practice your religion and/or culture. "Children understand that people are different," he says. "There's nothing wrong with families dealing honestly and straightforwardly with their cultural and religious differences. Just don't do it in a contrived or affected way in an effort to influence the child. But if what you practice and believe has been a part of your life, then don't hide it."

Show off elements of your culture and beliefs during holidays, he says. You can best do this through religious rituals, food, music, and folk tales.

In her excellent book, *The Essential Grandparent*, Dr. Lillian Carson writes:

> Developing children's religious, racial and cultural identity provides them with the building blocks for their identity, the knowledge of who they are. It gives them a sense of belonging to something greater than themselves. When you teach your grandchildren about your unique heritage, you are telling them about yourself. It's a way for them to get to know you. Grandparents have a right to tell their grandchildren who they are, with the parents' permission. When this is done in a non-judgmental way, you can have a tremendous positive influence.

First of all, face your own feelings and prejudices about the differences. The degree of difficulty this presents depends on deep-seated beliefs. Today we are learning the value of embracing diversity. It enriches our lives. You must proceed with great diplomacy so that you don't offend the parents when transmitting your grandchildren's heritage, by carefully considering what you say and how you say it. By accepting differences, you can bring harmony to the family and nurture mutual respect and love in the midst of ambiguity . . . This creates a situation that requires great tolerance and a need to appreciate and respect differences. It is a rich learning opportunity.

Multigenerational Households

According to the U.S. Census Bureau, there are four million multigenerational family households in the United States where the grandparents live under the same roof with two or more generations of descendants. In 65 percent of these households, the families live in the grandparents' home.

Whether your adult child and his or her family move into your home or you move into theirs, you can live harmoniously if you reach an understanding about the living arrangements beforehand.

"It's important, right at the very beginning to avoid unnecessary misunderstandings and frustrations by clarifying what each one expects of the other," says Nancy Covert, of the Penn State cooperative extension service. "In order to do this, a special time for discussion and decision-making should be set as soon as possible. It isn't always fair to live by 'my rules' or 'your rules.' When two households merge, it's better to clarify what is needed and expected of both by establishing new rules for the group to decide upon."

Hold a family session to iron out issues and avoid potential problems. Include any children who are old enough to contribute to the family discussion. "If the discussion is open, honest, and sensible, young children can feel a real sense of family security, gain self-esteem, and learn how to function as team players," says Covert.

Allowing every member to openly express his or her concerns and suggestions makes for a smoother-running household. "When you plan together, don't expect to agree on everything," she says. "You are individuals who have grown up in different eras, with different influences on your lives. These influences often affect how you feel about matters such as money, work, education, food, entertainment, and even religion. Time is needed to work through these differences and come to the best compromise when you cannot agree."

Moving in together can have its benefits, but it also can cause mixed emotions and financial strain, says Jane Mecum, of the Penn State cooperative extension service. "While it will be great to be around your grandchildren and be an active part of their lives, it can create conflicts. It is important to remember that each adult was living independently before and now each generation will begin to rely on one another."

Some household expenses will be reduced; others increased. Determining who pays for what is an important discussion before any move is made.

"Because there are three generations living together, ground rules will be important," says Mecum. "You may find yourself having more rules now than when you were raising your own children. Little items such as laundry, TV, company, curfews, meal times, discipline, decision-making, and privacy are a few things you will want to talk about. Rules can be changed as the generations blend together. If you are going to share a home with your adult children and grandchildren, you should have a role in important decisions, especially those that affect you directly.

"Constructively solving difficulties that arise when different generations live together will make it easier to share resources, enjoy each other's companionship, and overcome hardships. A clear understanding of roles and responsibilities together with a large dose of respect can make several generations together a functional and happy family unit."

Grandparents Raising Grandkids

Most grandparents raising grandchildren have taken on a labor of love they didn't choose. It chose them. In most cases, a complicated set of circumstances presented these nanas and papas with an unexpected challenge that they accepted—some happily, some reluctantly, some because they had to. At a time in their lives when they expected to be playing more tennis, opening a craft shop, or riding the back roads in their RV, they find themselves enmeshed in diapers, play groups, and PTA. Their free time is now spent battling the court system, social services departments, and health care providers.

They are parenting once again—and it isn't any easier. Less leisure, more laundry; less freedom, more chores; less money, more commotion. And through it all, they wish things had gone better for their kids and feel pangs of guilt because things haven't.

> **Butch Kellett, 47:** *"Starting over at this age, I've learned a lot about patience. It was rough at first [taking in his three-year-old grandson Tyler]."*

> **Kathy Kellett, 43:** *"When you get past the sadness, it's wonderful. We're lucky—not everyone is as excited to raise a grandchild."*

Today more than 4.5 million children in the United States live full-time with their grandparents, nearly double the number in 1980, according to the Census Bureau. In 2003, the bureau said that 2.4 million grandparents (including 1.5 million boomers) were the primary caregivers to their grandchildren, responsible for their basic needs such as food, shelter, and clothing. More than a third of these grandparents are caring for children whose parents don't live with them.

"Grandparent caregivers may face legal and social problems," says Amy Goyer, director of AARP's Grandparent Information Center (GIC). "They may lack support and respite services, affordable housing and/or access to medical services, and insurance coverage of medical expenses for the grandchildren. Investigating and resolving legal questions around custody, guardianship, or adoption are major challenges. Without legal status, grandparents may not be able to enroll their grandchildren in school, have access to their grandchildren's school records, or make medical decisions for them.

"These problems are exacerbated by the demands of becoming a parent again. Additionally, some of these grandchildren have special medical or learning needs that may put further financial and emotional strain on the family."

According to the GIC, grandparents are raising their children because of parental substance abuse (44 percent of the cases); child abuse, neglect, or abandonment (28 percent); teenage pregnancy (11 percent); death or divorce of a parent (9 percent); and other reasons including parental unemployment, imprisonment, or illness (8 percent).

"Depending on the age of the children at the time they're dropped off at their grandparent's door, they arrive already depressed, angry, resentful, frightened, mistrustful, or in overall emotional turmoil," says Sally Houtman, M.S., author of *To Grandma's House, We . . . Stay.* "The older the children, the more emotional baggage they'll have had a chance to collect and will no doubt pack for their journey to your home.

"Children of alcohol- and drug-addicted parents, as well as children of parents who are unstable for other reasons, will bring with them more than their share of physical and emotional problems. Some have been born suffering the aftermath of parental chemical abuse, which can have a wide variety of long-lasting effects. These may take the form of physical disabilities, mental or emotional disturbances, or perceptual, learning, or attention deficits. So on top of becoming parents without preparation, the grandparents who inherit these children also inherit the legacy of the parent's poor judgments, negligence, impulsiveness, and indulgences."

> **Nana on the Net:** *"I love my grandkids, but I wish I could have been just a regular grandparent and spoil them and then send them home."*

This is such a complex issue that it goes beyond the scope of this book. However, according to experts, if you are about to face this situation, consider doing the following:

- Find a support group in your area so you can talk to other grandparents. (Several national organizations are listed in the appendix.)

- Talk to social agencies and organizations to find out what assistance may be available to you. Temporary Assistance to Needy Families offers financial help to families with low incomes. The money comes from the federal government, but the states run the program. Contact the department of social or human services in your county to find out about the rules in your state.
- Expect to face many major adjustments in your life that will affect your lifestyle, finances, marriage, career, and friendships.
- Be prepared to improvise in the face of unusual and sometimes difficult situations.
- Understand your legal options such as temporary or full custody, foster care, guardianship, or adoption. When custody is established by law, grandparents gain rights and benefits not offered with other caregiving arrangements. These benefits include health insurance, social services, government financial assistance, housing, and school enrollment.

Sherry (Grammy) Johnson: *"I was seen as 'interfering' when advocating for my grandchildren's basic needs like baths, sleep, and proper food. It was easier for me just to have them live with me."*

If you already are raising your grandchild, consider these words of wisdom from the experts:

- Don't lie to your grandchild about her parents. Kids are capable of handling the truth. No matter how well-meaning it may seem to fib, lies require high maintenance and they eventually come back to haunt you.
- Keep in mind that the child is not responsible for the situation and should not be put in a position of being blamed or shamed.
- If you're taking on the role of the full-time parent, you must parent. You can't be just the grandparent anymore. That means you have to set the limits, establish the rules, and hand out the discipline.
- Take pride in what you do. You are rescuing a child from a terrible situation and providing her with a loving, stable environment.

- Try to be compassionate, supportive, and flexible to help your grandchild work through the loss of her parents.
- If you're dealing with a troubled child, allow her to express her anger, which is part of the healing process. But also help her learn new ways to communicate and to cope with the situation.
- Don't compare this situation to your first parenting experience. Everything is different, including you, the times, the circumstances, and the child.

Nana on the Net: *"I had various grandchildren for days, weeks, and months at a time. I provided almost all of their needs, including paying for their mother's and her boyfriend's rent, bikes, and vehicle. But the drugs and alcohol are fighting me for dominance in my grandchildren's lives."*

"Children raised by grandparents long to have a healthy and loving parent besides their grandparents," says Dr. Kornhaber. "Mature, sensitive grandparents are aware of these dynamics and should defer their own needs to those of the child. It is inherent in the grandparent role to move in and out of being a nurturer, mentor, role model, playmate, and caretaker."

Many grandparents who raise children claim it's another opportunity to enjoy a close relationship. They often report a greater sense of purpose, according to a study conducted by Margaret Jendrek of Miami University in Ohio. In the Grandparent Study, more than 90 percent of the grandparents raising grandchildren stated that doing so has given new meaning to their own lives. Nevertheless, most of them acknowledged having mixed feelings.

"Some grandparents resent the disruption in their lives caused by their grandchildren's needs for time and attention," reports Dr. Kornhaber. "Grandparents raising debilitated grandchildren—such as those with fetal alcohol syndrome, malnourishment, health, behavioral, or learning problems—may resent the extra care required. Others express bitterness that all too often society's institutions do not support their efforts with adequate funding, health care, and social agencies.

"Despite the negative emotions and various problems that may arise, caregiving grandparents feel useful and also derive satisfaction from knowing they are rescuing their grandchildren. Such caregivers in the Grandparent Study said they had increased energy and interest in daily life and noticed an improvement in mood since they started raising their grandchildren. These caregivers report they cope better if they have a family support network."

Another study said grandparents deal with the pressures of raising grandchildren by using prayer, meditating, having fun with the grandchild, or changing their perspective of the situation so that this burden becomes a mission and a challenge.

Many grandparents raising grandchildren experience a sense of deprivation, says family therapist Lenora M. Poe, Ph.D., author of *Black Grandparents as Parents*. They feel deprived of a positive relationship with their own children (the birth parents). "Many of them grieve over the emotional death of their sons or daughters. Some of them try to rationalize away their grief by disowning their children," she says.

In an article for the *GIC Newsletter*, Poe writes:

> The grandparents feel that they can no longer trust their adult sons and daughters, and they often wonder whether they are to blame for their children's behaviors. Having "failed" as parents with their own children, they question what they can improve this time, and wonder if they will "fail" a second time around. They also wonder how to counter the continuing negative influences of their children on their grandchildren. Throughout all this, they feel ambivalence toward both their children and their grandchildren—whom they love on the one hand, and resent on the other. Because of the love that these grandparents have for their adult sons and daughters, they often have a difficult time setting appropriate limits and boundaries for them. Thus, when a son or daughter shows up (perhaps on probation from prison), a grandparent's authority with the grandchildren may quickly be undermined by the son's or daughter's disruptive behavior. In most cases, the grandparent does not have legal

custody or guardianship of the children, so the son or daughter has the legal right to arbitrarily remove the children or, in some cases, to walk off with the monthly welfare check and spend it on drugs.

Some grandparents have attempted to deal with this last intrusion by involving the birth parents in some of the grandchildren's daily routines, such as homework, after-school activities, or family dinners. These grandparents hope that this involvement will encourage the birth parents to begin taking responsibility for their lives. When this fails . . . grandparents may have to exclude their son or daughter from the home . . . This is an extremely painful moment for a grandparent, but sometimes there is simply no other option.

Nana on the Net: *"I'm taking action in the interests of my grandchildren. There will be no more bouncing them around. I am prepared to raise them—and to face the results this will have on my adult daughters who'll likely drug themselves into oblivion."*

No matter what kind of nontraditional family your grandchild might live in—single parent, gay parents, interracial marriage, grandparent-headed household—it's not necessarily a bad situation, says Alan Acock, professor and chair of the Department of Human Development and Family Services at Oregon State University. He and David Demo, professor and chair of the department of Human Development and Family Studies at the University of North Carolina-Greensboro, conducted a study of adolescents. The researchers found that the makeup of a household matters less than does the level of family conflict, income, and education. The less the hostility and the higher the household income and education, the better the conditions are for the child. Most important is the quality of time a custodial adult spends with the child.

"Family dynamics are far more important than family composition," says Acock. "You can have a secure, stable, nurturing environment with one parent or two."

Walk Right In

When Your Grandchild Visits

W

HEN OUR GRANDSONS CHAD AND DANNY come to visit, we put our
life on hold and go into what we call our Grandkid Mode. We spring
into action and prepare ourselves and our house for their arrival—or,
more aptly, their invasion.

First, we reschedule or cancel any social plans and other appointments, and we inform our friends we'll be out of the loop during our
grandsons' stay. Most everything comes to a halt, including a few days
of work because we try to create as much free time as possible for them.
Total focus goes to Chad and Danny.

Mentally, we know what will happen to our house. It will be trashed:
Toys scattered everywhere—under the dining room table, behind the
curtains, between the couch cushions. Sticky fingerprints on walls, windows, and appliances. Juicy Juice on chairs, floors, and carpets. We
accept the fact that the moment they enter our house, all sense of order
walks out. No matter what plans we make, we are prepared to call an
audible and change them because, with kids, you just never know.

We pull out the grandkids' boxes. One box contains picture books;
another has art supplies, including butcher paper, crayons, markers,
watercolors, and paste; one is full of videos; and another has simple
games, puzzles, and cards. Then we bring out the toy box. Instead of
one made of brightly-colored molded plastic, ours is a maple blanket
bench that fits in with our decor. Although it was designed to hold
blankets, we use it to store toys and sports equipment that we've col-
lected from friends and relatives. The lid has a child-safety hinge so it
won't fall down when opened.

When Chad and Danny were toddlers, we applied the "hide everything" philosophy. Before their visit, we would sweep through the

house like frenzied burglars and gather all the breakable or unsafe items that we didn't want them to touch. We put these things out of their reach and sight. That way we didn't have to fret over the fate of breakable objects and we didn't have to say "no" to the boys so many times.

Some grandparents leave their possessions out and try to teach their grandkids how to respect the items. But that takes alertness, composure, and effort on your part, and it only works if your grandchild visits frequently. But be prepared for the inevitable accidents. If there's an object that's priceless to you, put it away during the visit.

When our grandsons were no longer toddlers, we designated an open space in the lower level of the house a "Kid Zone." They know it's a place where they can drag out their toys and games and basically trash the area. They don't have to worry about picking up all their things every night.

> **Sue (Nana) Crawford:** *"When the grandchildren come, we stay in the family room, which can be closed off from the rest of the house. It's child-proofed and we have all the toys in there. My living room and dining room are full of crystal and other fragile things. Having one room a mess is easier to clean up and to get back to normal."*

The grandparents' house should be a second home for the grandkids—a getaway to explore, rummage through family memorabilia, encounter the unexpected, and celebrate holidays with the whole family. It should have a closet full of children's books and favorite games. (Make sure you practice so you can play the games with them.) The refrigerator and pantry should be stocked with the grandkids' favorite food and snacks.

Get an old dresser and designate a drawer for each grandkid. Inside put fun items such as old clothes, hats and purses, junk jewelry, puzzles, a magnifying glass, magnets, and dozens of inexpensive things that you can find at a drugstore or flea market. Let the grandkids know they each have their very own drawer. When they visit, they'll eagerly open it to see what's new inside. Your challenge will be to change the contents as the kids get older.

> **Kathryn:** *"I don't fret about the crumbs on the floor and fingerprints on the windows when they're visiting. I do a major housecleaning after they leave. I confess that sometimes I've deliberately left their handprints on the windows for several days because they're a cute reminder of the boys' visit."*

Childproofing Your Home

When our first grandchild, Chad, was three months old, he came to our house for his first visit. We had forgotten how much preparation is needed to provide a healthy, safe environment for an infant.

After reading the safety guidelines from the Consumer Product Safety Commission (CPSC), we discovered that potential hazards lurked in every corner of our house. Adding to our concern were these sobering stats from the CPSC: More children die in home accidents than from all childhood diseases combined. And more than one-third of all potentially harmful or fatal childhood poisonings occur in the homes of children's *grandparents*.

Before baby Chad arrived at our house, we got down on all fours and took an infant's-eye-view of each room to check for any dangers. We discovered a cat toy lodged under the couch but within a child's reach and a ballpoint pen inadvertently left as a bookmark in a magazine on the coffee table.

To safeguard your home for the little one, you must be as diligent and vigilant as Sergeant Joe Friday. Too often, when young children visit, we tend to worry about what the kids might do to our things rather than what the things might do to the kids. Just ask yourself, what's more precious to you—your Limoges collection or your grandchildren? Evaluate the environment of your home in light of their safety.

Some grandparents are so concerned about the safety issue that they are willing to pay professionals who will childproof their homes.

"You're constantly sweating it when you have very young children around," admits Barbara Bowman, president of the Erikson Institute.

"You must be more vigilant than ever. I found I'm much more careful with my granddaughter than I ever was with my own child. I would die if anything would happen to her on my watch."

If you don't already have one, get a cordless phone and keep it with you when you're watching or bathing your grandchild. That way, if you get a phone call, she never has to leave your sight. Let's face it, no matter what precautions you take to childproof your home, absolutely nothing is safer for your grandchild than you keeping your eye on her at all times.

If you want to gain more confidence in yourself as a baby-sitter, take a Red Cross course on infant and child CPR and standard first aid. Heed the following guidelines suggested by the CPSC and other safety-conscious organizations, including AARP's Grandparent Information Center. Most of these tips involve common sense, but they are helpful reminders. (Hey, airline pilots go through a checklist before every flight, so why shouldn't nanas and papas go through one before every grandchild visit?)

Around the house:

- Place sturdy safety gates at the top and bottom of the stairs. Gates with small diamond-shaped openings are best since they can't entrap small fingers like accordion-style gates.

- Keep all insect spray, weed killers, gasoline, paint products, bleaches, soaps, detergents, oven and drain cleaners, polishes, fabric softeners, bluing agents, and stain treatment sprays in their original containers and in a secure cabinet.

- Keep all thin plastic wrapping materials, such as dry cleaning, produce, or trash bags out of your grandchild's reach. Never use thin plastic material to cover mattresses or pillows because the plastic film can cling to her face, causing suffocation.

- Guard against electrical shocks by covering unused outlets with safety caps.

Michelle (Grammy) Davies: *"Nothing is toddler-proof. Before my two-year-old grandson came over to my new house, I covered the electrical outlets. He wasn't there thirty minutes when he brought me a handful of outlet covers."*

- Keep your grandchild away from open windows and screens to prevent a fall. Screens are designed to keep insects out, not kids in. Avoid placing furniture near windows so she can't climb out the window.
- Lock lower windows and block them so they can't be opened more than six inches.
- Always use restraining straps with an infant carrier seat. Don't place the carrier seat on any soft, unstable surfaces.
- If you have a swimming pool, install a fence or barrier surrounding all four sides with self-closing and self-latching gates. If the house is part of the barrier, all doors leading from the house to the pool should be protected with an alarm and locks.
- Consider using safety netting on decks and balconies to prevent falls.
- Use safety latches for kitchen, bathroom, and workshop cabinets.
- Make sure your floors are smooth and have nonskid surfaces. Rugs should be skid-proof.

Glen Ecklund: *"Watch out for wastebaskets! Ours is locked away under the sink, but Ethan still managed to transfer a couple of spoons from the dishwasher to it. We were lucky to notice them while taking out the trash. However Madeleine's keys are long gone."*

- Make sure pipes, radiators, fireplaces, wood-burning stoves, and other hot surfaces can't be reached by your grandchild.
- Cushion fireplace edges with commercial corner guards.
- Never drink coffee, tea, or a cup containing other hot liquid when holding your grandchild.

- Never use open buckets as diaper pails or leave open buckets containing liquids where children can reach them. The containers pose a drowning hazard.

- Never tie pacifiers or other items around the baby's neck. Cords and ribbons can become tightly twisted, or can catch on crib corner posts or other protrusions, causing strangulation.

- Keep your grandchild away from common toxic houseplants such as daffodils, delphinium, dieffenbachia, hydrangea, philodendrons, poinsettias, lily of the valley, caladium, and foxglove. For a complete list, contact your local poison control center.

- Use latches on lower drawers of a dresser to ensure that your grandchild doesn't open them and use them as steps, causing it to tip over. You can also use angle braces or anchors to secure furniture to a wall.

- Make sure all interior doors can be easily unlocked and opened from the outside in case your grandchild locks herself inside a room.

Diane Willis: *"People should be really careful of the rubber tips on doorstops. I couldn't believe Nick crawled all around the house and stripped them off every single doorstop. We then removed the doorstops from the wall because the sharp points where the rubber tip goes could injure Nick."*

- If you let your grandchild play outside, first check the area and clean up any debris, sharp objects, or pet droppings.

- Have handy the phone number of your local poison control center, a pediatrician, and other emergency numbers.

- Have first-aid materials and simple medications on hand, such as Band-Aids, antibacterial salve, thermometer, antidiarrhea preparations, and ice packs.

- Obtain an emergency medical release form giving you the authority to approve medical care for your grandchild if the parents are away. (For more details, see the chapter on grandparents' legal issues.)

In the bathroom:

- Store electrical devices such as curling irons, hair dryers, and razors away from water and from your grandchild's reach. Make sure they're disconnected when not in use.
- Keep cleaning products, disinfectants, cosmetics, powders, fingernail preparations, hair care products, mouthwash, and medicine locked in a cabinet or out of your grandchild's reach. Remember: child-resistant packaging is not necessarily childproof.
- Don't throw shaving products like disposable razors and other potentially dangerous objects into the wastebasket. Wrap them in toilet paper and put them directly into the garbage.
- Keep all perfumes, cosmetics, powders, and sachets out of your grandchild's reach.

Kathryn: *"When Chad was fifteen months old, he managed to lock himself in the bathroom at home. Our daughter Allison was worried that he would somehow fall in the toilet or hurt himself in some way. After five tense minutes, Dan, our son-in-law, finally sprang the old lock with a screwdriver. They found Chad covered from head to toe in toilet paper."*

- Set the water heater temperature at between 110 and 120 degrees Fahrenheit to help prevent scald burns. Always check bathwater temperature with your wrist or elbow before putting your grandchild in to bathe. If you want to be supersafe, buy an antiscalding device, which ranges in price from $6 to $30.
- At bath time, fill the tub with just enough water to cover your grandchild's legs.
- Never leave your grandchild alone or with a youngster in the bath even for a few seconds. If the phone rings and it's not a cordless phone, don't answer it. It can't be as important as the safety of your grandchild.
- And for all you grandfathers, here's the hardest safety tip of all: Keep the toilet seat—and cover—down. (And, for extra safety, install a toilet seat latch.)

In the nursery:

- Put your grandchild to sleep on her back or side in a crib with a firm, flat mattress and no soft bedding underneath her. Studies indicate this will reduce the risk of suffocation and Sudden Infant Death Syndrome (SIDS).
- Never let the infant sleep on an adult bed, waterbed, or bunk bed because she can fall out or become trapped between the bed and the wall and suffocate.
- Never place the baby's crib or furniture near cords for window blinds or curtains. An infant can strangle on the loop of the cord.
- Keep cords out of reach by tying them to themselves or by using clamps, clothespins, cleats, or tie-down devices. Also, consider tying or hanging cords at or near the top of the window coverings.
- To prevent choking, take rattles, squeeze toys, teethers, and other toys out of the crib when the baby sleeps.
- Remove all crib toys that are strung across the crib when your grandchild is beginning to push up on her hands and knees or is five months old, whichever occurs first.
- Remove bibs and necklaces whenever you put the baby in a crib or playpen.
- Always lock the side rail in its raised position whenever you place the child in the crib. As soon as she can stand up, adjust the mattress to its lowest position and remove the bumper pads. Also, remove any large toys—an active toddler will use any-thing to climb out of the crib.
- When the child reaches three feet in height, she has outgrown the crib and should sleep in a bed.

In the kitchen:

- When the baby is in a high chair, always use all safety straps to prevent her from climbing out, falling, or sliding under the tray. Don't leave her alone for even a few seconds.
- Keep the high chair far enough away from a table, counter, wall, or other surface so that she can't use them to push off.

Bob (Boppy) Giovanni: *"Beware of oven doors. When our granddaughter Gillian was about two, she walked by the hot oven and yanked open the door. I hadn't run across the room that fast since I grabbed the last beer at a frat party."*

- Use your stove's back burners and turn the pot handles inward whenever possible.
- Keep your grandchild away from tablecloths, so she can't pull down hot foods or liquids on herself.

Gran Nan: *"We learned the hard way not to have tablecloths around when our granddaughter Bree visits. When she was sixteen months old, she yanked on a tablecloth to pull herself up and knocked over a vase that conked her on the head."*

- Keep all countertop appliances, such as the toaster or coffeepot, away from the edge. Keep them unplugged when not in use.
- Lock up household cleaning products, knives, matches, and plastic bags or keep them on shelves in upper cabinets.

Gramma Kay: *"Look in your kitchen drawers. Besides the obvious like knives, you should put boxes of foil and plastic wrap out of reach. Our grandson Trevor cut his hand on the sharp edge of one of those boxes. I felt so sick to my stomach because his safety was my responsibility and I let him down. It was hard for me to face his parents."*

Handling Food

When feeding your infant grandchild, first test all warmed foods for a comfortable eating temperature before serving.

Heating baby food in a microwave is convenient, but many experts advise against it because it often leaves hot spots in the food that can burn your grandchild's mouth. If you do use a microwave, make sure you stir the food from the center out after heating to ensure that the temperature is even. Bottles of milk should never be microwaved because of hot spots. It's best to run the bottles under warm tap water (but never in boiling water).

When your grandchild begins eating solid foods, between four and eight months old, don't give her small, hard foods. They could lodge in her throat and cause her to suffocate. Wait until she's older or ask her parent when it's safe for her to eat nuts, chunky peanut butter, whole grapes, fruits with seeds or pits, breads with large pieces of grain, hard candy, popcorn, small slices of raw vegetables, and whole hot dogs.

Newborns and children under one year old are more vulnerable to food poisoning because of undeveloped immune systems. Even a small dose of harmful bacteria can make a tiny baby sick. Don't give her left-over formula or milk from a previous feeding because harmful bacteria from the baby's mouth can get into the formula where it can grow and multiply even after refrigeration and reheating.

If using commercial baby foods, check to see that the safety button on the lid is down. If the jar lid doesn't "pop" when opened, don't use it. Discard jars with chipped glass or rusty lids. Don't feed the baby straight from a jar if you plan on saving some of the baby food. Saliva on the spoon can contaminate the remaining food. Transfer food from the jar to a bowl before feeding the baby.

Honey is a no-no for babies because of the potential of infant botulism. Honey should not be given to, or used in foods for, infants under the age of one. Below this age, infants don't have adequate stomach acid to inactivate botulinal spores.

Remember how you let your kids eat raw cookie dough or raw cake batter? Experts now say that's risky because the raw eggs in the mixture can lead to food-borne illness from salmonella poisoning.

Careful hand-washing with soap is one of the best ways to stop germs from spreading. As soon as your grandchild can understand, stress hand-washing after going to the bathroom and before eating.

Baby bottles, nipples, screw caps, and covers all should be carefully washed, air dried, and stored until needed. Filled bottles and open cans of formula should be kept in the refrigerator. Filled bottles should be used within twenty-four hours, open cans within forty-eight hours. To prevent bacterial growth, don't leave the baby's bottle out of the refrigerator for longer than two hours and throw away any formula left after a feeding.

Pets

Your dog, cat, or pet gecko might not be accustomed to the noise and actions of your grandchild. Honestly assess the animal's personality to see how well it can tolerate the intrusion of a young child. If your pet can't handle the situation, put it outside, in the basement, or in a room during the visit. Otherwise, use care and patience when introducing your pet to her. If your grandchild is old enough, teach her how to approach the animal. Never leave her alone with any dog, cat, or other pet.

Also, be sure you store the pet food out of your grandchild's reach. And don't leave any out in a bowl on the floor. Some kinds of dry food are perfect choking size for a crawling baby.

Baby Equipment

If your infant grandchild visits you, you need at the very least a crib or playpen, high chair, car seat, and stroller.

It's often impractical for the parents to lug all that baby equipment, especially when flying, so you have several choices: You can buy used items at swap meets or garage sales; purchase new equipment; borrow stuff from friends or neighbors, or drag out the things you last stored in the attic during the Ford administration.

That last choice can be a problem because much of the equipment we used when our kids were little is considered too dangerous today. In fact, after hearing tips from experts and seeing the latest products for infants, you wonder how our kids survived babyhood. Virtually everything we used back then—the wind-up swing with chain link supports, the wobbly walkers, the wide-slatted cribs—is not only obsolete but a potential child-maimer or killer.

When choosing used or new baby equipment, check for poor construction, instability, missing parts, and excessive wear. Most manufacturers have a toll-free number and will offer replacement parts and instructions. Avoid getting equipment that has any exposed screws, bolts, or fasteners with sharp edges or points, and scissorslike mechanisms that could crush fingers.

If you're wondering if a new or used product is safe to use, look for a tag or sticker that says it is certified by the Juvenile Products Manufacturers Association (JPMA) or the American Society for Testing and Materials (ASTM). Stringent standards have been developed for high chairs, playpens, walkers, strollers, gates and enclosures, full-size cribs, portable hook-on chairs, and other products for babies and toddlers.

To check for any recalls, go to www.recalls.gov.

Crib

Have you been saving your children's old crib for your grandchildren? Unless it meets national safety standards, keep it in the attic as an heirloom or use it for kindling. Each year, according to the CPSC, about fifty babies suffocate or strangle when they become trapped between broken crib parts or in cribs with older, unsafe designs.

> **Ohio Congressman Dave Hobson:** *"I learned that the crib my three children used was actually considered unsafe for infants so we bought a new one in time for our next grandchildren's visit."*

According to the CPSC, a safe crib has:

- no missing, loose, broken, or improperly-installed screws, brackets, or other hardware on the crib or the mattress support
- no missing slats
- no more than 2⅜ inches between crib slats so the baby's body can't fit through the slats. (Here's an easy way to measure: Try passing an upright soda can between the slats. If the can goes through, the slats are spaced too far apart, so get rid of the crib.)
- a firm, snug-fitting mattress so the baby can't get trapped between the mattress and the side of the crib. (You should not be able to get more than two adult fingers in the space between the mattress and the sides of the crib.)

- no corner posts over ¹⁄₁₆ of an inch above the end panels (unless they are over sixteen inches high for a canopy), which could snag the baby's clothes and strangle her
- no cutout areas on the headboard or footboard that could trap the baby's head
- a mattress support that doesn't easily pull apart from the corner posts so the baby can't get trapped between the mattress and crib; mattress support hangers should be secured by closed hooks
- drop-side latches that can't be released by a child
- no cracked or peeling paint
- no splinters or rough edges

Safety seat

During your grandchild's visit, you'll need a child safety seat. Many hospitals rent seats and several auto insurance companies subsidize new purchases. Although more expensive than regular seats, convertible seats—which face toward the rear for infants and face forward for toddlers—can be a better buy in the long run.

Most states have a child passenger protection law requiring small children (usually up to age four or forty pounds) to ride in approved child safety seats. The best way to transport your grandchild is in a child safety seat in the rear middle seat of your car.

From birth until your grandchild weighs twenty pounds, use an infant or convertible seat facing the rear of the vehicle to provide the most protection. Over the age of one or from twenty to forty pounds, use a convertible seat or forward-facing seat. Children ages four to eight and over forty pounds should use a belt-positioning booster seat.

Don't place a safety seat in the front seat of a vehicle that has an airbag on the passenger side. If it's necessary to put a child in the front seat, make sure the airbag system is turned off and the seat is moved back as far as possible.

If you're planning on buying a new car, consider getting one with built-in child seats. Most vehicles manufactured since 2000 are equipped with LATCH, or Lower Anchors and Tethers for Children, a new system to make using car seats easier and safer. Instead of trying to secure your car seat with the car's own seat belts, you can strap it to a top tether anchor and lower, side anchorage points.

Other baby products

Here are more tips from the CPSC:

- Don't use a framed back carrier before your grandchild is four or five months old. By then, the baby's neck will able to withstand jolts and not sustain an injury. It should have enough depth to support her back. The leg openings should be small enough to prevent her from slipping out but big enough to avoid chafing her legs.

- Bicycle carriers should not be used before your grandchild is one year old. Developmentally, children are just learning to sit unsupported around nine months old. It's not until this age that infants have developed sufficient bone mass and muscle tone to enable them to sit unsupported with their backs straight.

- Never place a carrier seat on soft surfaces such as beds or sofas. The carrier seat may tip over and the baby may strangle or suffocate. If the carrier seat does not already have nonskid feet, attach rough-surfaced adhesive strips to the underside. Always use the safety belts and keep them snug. A carrier seat is not always an infant car seat, and should never be used in a vehicle unless it is labeled for that purpose.

- Make sure the portable, umbrella-type stroller pushes smoothly and easily and has a three-point safety strap. If you live in a sunny climate, use a canopy.

- Look for high chairs that have two safety straps—a waist strap and a crotch strap. Never depend upon the feeding tray to restrain or protect your grandchild. Instead, secure the straps.

- Don't use a playpen with holes in the netting larger than ¼ inch or with wooden slats further than 2⅜ inches apart. (Try the soda can test.) With a wood playpen, check for any missing or loose staples. And make sure it's properly opened and locked.

- Don't use a mesh-sided portable crib with a side left down. Such a position can pose a serious hazard because the mesh forms a loose pocket into which your infant grandchild can roll and suffocate. Also, don't add a pillow or a mattress that is deeper than one inch.
- If your grandchild is in a baby walker, keep her away from areas where there are uneven floors such as carpet edges or raised thresholds that may cause the walker to tip over.

Toys and toy chest

- Check that all playthings you give your grandchild are safe, especially hand-me-downs and garage-sale specials.
- Throw away any toys that have lead-based paint, removable parts less than 1¼ inches long, or that have sharp edges, corners, or protrusions.
- Keep small objects out of your grandchild's reach. Check to see that toys have not broken or come apart at the seams, exposing small pellets that might be swallowed or inhaled. Even such common items as coins, pins, buttons, or small batteries can choke a child. If you're wondering if a toy or object is small enough, try dropping it into a tube from an empty roll of toilet paper. If the object falls through, then it is potentially dangerous.
- When choosing toys, look for labels that give age recommendations such as "Recommended for Children Three to Five Years Old." Some toys or games that are safe for older children may contain small parts that are hazardous in a younger child's hands.
- Be aware of the dangers of balloons whether they are inflated or not. Never allow a child to put his or her mouth on an inflated balloon. Uninflated or broken balloons are choking hazards. If a balloon breaks, throw the broken pieces away immediately. More children have suffocated on uninflated balloons and broken balloon pieces than any other type of toy, according to the CPSC.
- Avoid toys that young children can break apart by twisting, pulling, or banging. Broken toys can be dangerous, especially if

the broken pieces have jagged or sharp plastic or metal edges. Toys with glass, which can break easily, are not intended for children under age eight.

- Avoid toys that make loud noises. They can damage hearing and frighten babies and very young children. Test the toy next to your own ear to see if it would be too loud for children.

- If you have saved old toys for your grandchildren or bought used toys, be sure they are safe and in good working condition. Older toys that were manufactured before current safety standards could pose risks for children using them. You might want to check the CPSC Web site (www.cpsc.gov) to see if it has safety warnings about your old toy.

- If a toy chest, trunk, or other container for storing toys has a free-falling lid, remove the lid. Otherwise it can accidentally drop on your grandchild's head or neck. Look for a chest that has supports to hold the lid open at any position, or choose one with sliding panels or a lightweight, removable lid. Another remedy is to get a spring-loaded lid-support device that will keep a lid from falling on your grandchild or from closing and trapping her inside. This device costs about $7.50 and should be used on all chests or trunks. Also, make sure the toy chest doesn't have a latch but does have air holes in the side in case she falls in.

Ken Meinken: *"I used to be a volunteer EMT. One of my early life squad runs was on a young child [put to bed for a nap] who got out of bed and crawled into the toy box and fell asleep there. He never awoke. Despite our CPR efforts and the hospital's efforts, he couldn't be revived. Although it's been fifteen years and a thousand other emergency runs have come and gone, I still shudder every time I see an unventilated toy box in a store."*

I've Got to Get a Message to You

The Long-Distance Grandparent

IF YOU'RE A LONG-DISTANCE GRANDPARENT, you can still enjoy a meaningful relationship with your grandkid and play an important role in his life. It doesn't matter whether you live on Alaska's North Slope and he hails from the Florida Keys. You can be close to him.

The secret is to promote yourself with a Cassius Clay vigor. Long before he became Muhammad Ali, the boxer made his impact on the world by brashly hyping himself. (Okay, so he had a wicked right, too.) He refused to let the world ignore him.

Don't let your faraway grandchild ignore you—and don't you ignore him. Despite the distance, you can make an impact in his life in dozens of different ways, showing him how much he means to you. With today's technology, it's easier than ever for you to stay in touch with your grandkid and display your love, concern, values, sense of humor, and family history.

"There is absolutely no excuse for out of sight, out of mind," declares sociologist and family expert Susan Newman. "You have e-mail, faxes, videophones, and telephone."

It might take more effort, imagination, and creativity to grandparent from a different state, but you can be nearly as effective as the grandparent who lives down the street. The key is to keep in touch on a regular basis with your grandchild as you learn about him and he learns about you. Making your presence (in spirit) known strengthens your ties with him and reminds him that he is in your thoughts every day.

> **Jackie Quiram:** *"Being a long-distance grandmother means taking every opportunity to make a connection. Over the years, what you share together with grandchildren adds up to lots of rich experiences."*

It's a whole lot easier to pull off if you have a decent relationship with the parents. If they don't help, your efforts to stay close to your grandchild are much harder. From the start, your adult children need to know how important it is for you to stay in touch with him. The parents need to talk about you (hopefully in a positive light) to him. They need to constantly reinforce in the child how much you care about him. Nag the parents to help your promotion campaign. Use guilt, bribery, threats—whatever. Hey, this is your grandchild connection. It can't work very well without the parents' cooperation.

Through phone, letters, videos, e-mail, and other means, you can share your world with your grandchild. It sets the stage for those wonderful times when you're finally face-to-face with him. You won't have to get reacquainted because you aren't meeting as strangers; you're just enhancing an already blossoming relationship.

"Make your presence known in ways so simple that they'll become automatic," says Newman. "Small gestures frequently are the most meaningful."

E-Mail

Get online with your distant grandchild.

If you both have computers and access to e-mail, you can enjoy almost instantaneous communication. You can exchange daily messages, riddles, and jokes and play a variety of online games with your grandchild, depending on his age. Many Internet service providers offer instant messaging so you can swap correspondence in real time.

Today, children are learning to use the computers by the time they start preschool. As one social scientist said, "Boomers' grandkids are the first generation to be raised with a mouse in one hand and a bottle in the other." At the age of three, our grandsons were able to play some basic computer games by themselves. And although we'd like to think they are brilliant kids, the truth is that their friends were operating computers with equal dexterity at preschool age. The Internet allows us to send silly jokes, animated greeting cards, and simple messages to them, and for them to practice their spelling.

The computer offers grandparents unprecedented opportunities to live a fuller and more influential life with their grandchildren, says Dr. Arthur Kornhaber. "Your ability to be computer literate will exponentially augment your grandparent power.

"With e-mail you can keep in close touch with family members and, because of the ability to communicate in an ongoing manner, become a part of their everyday lives—no matter how far you live from one another. This idea of being able to knit family ties over distances is one of the happiest—and unexpected—findings of our own research in this field. Your computer can help you become the heart of your family more than ever before. Your options for creativity will be infinite."

Stan (Papa) Twilliger: *"I picked up a children's joke book at the store and most every day when I'm in the office, I e-mail my grandson Michael a joke. His mom works at home so she finds the joke on her e-mail and reads it to him. He knows it's from Papa. His mom often e-mails me back with a comment or some funny thing that Michael said or did in preschool or at home."*

Harry (Papa) Yeatts: *"Though our granddaughter is too young to read e-mail, her mom uses it to let us know the little things our granddaughter is up to. And we ask our daughter to pass on our love and to ask her questions. This way we get to keep up with daily happenings. Also, our daughter and son-in-law record our granddaughter's storytelling and singing on their computer and e-mail it to us. It makes a fine start-up/exit sound file."*

Use the Internet to download and/or forward pictures, cute messages, and cartoons to your grandchild. Try sending electronic personalized greeting cards to him. In most cases, it doesn't cost anything to e-mail a personalized e-card. The Internet is chock-full of services offering free e-cards. To find these services, go to your search engine and type in "electronic greeting cards" or "e-cards."

You can design and customize e-cards using various multimedia shareware and freeware programs that let you use your own message and voice. Many such programs contain graphics with built-in animation, synthesized speech, music, sound, and text/graphic buttons. You can download these programs through the Internet or through the software library of your online service.

You might consider creating your own personal Web page where you or your grandchild's parents can keep your far-flung relatives up-to-date on what's going on in everyone's lives. It's another way to help your grandchild grasp the concept of being connected with family members from all over the country (or world, for that matter). Many online services offer their subscribers a way to build their own free home page. If you want to make a more creative Web site, you can buy special software or sign up with a network of personal home pages that will build and store your personal Web site on its domain for a relatively modest annual fee.

Moms and stay-at-home dads are "blogging," (a term derived from Web log). Bloggers are those who write regular, often daily, musings or diary entries on their personal Web site for all to read. Many bloggers include pictures of their children. Although the entire Internet world has access to these blogs, it's still another way that grandparents can stay connected with the day-to-day activities of their adult children and grandchildren.

> **Mommy blogger Megan Morrone:** *"Blogging is one way I communicate with [her daughter] Annabella's grandparents. I didn't start out doing it for them. Annabella was crying and I was rocking her and thinking that there must be millions of other moms out there like me home alone, so I started writing on my Web page [www.jumpingmonkeys.com] about my experiences with motherhood. I put up cute pictures of her. It's so easy and I enjoy it because I like to write.*
>
> *"Her grandparents love it because they live so far away in other states, so they check my site every day. Blogging has become something more for them, to show them what's going on in my life and Annabella's."*

Digital Cameras

Digital cameras allow you to see excellent color pictures of your long-distance grandchild on your computer within minutes after they were shot. They are as easy to use as conventional point-and-shoot film cameras, and the costs have come down considerably over the last few years.

Digital cameras have a built-in liquid crystal display that lets you immediately see what you've just shot. And unlike film cameras, if you don't like the results, you can delete the pictures. The picture-editing software that comes with these cameras lets you easily correct for such shutterbug problems as red-eye, underexposure, or color defects. Once you get the hang of the software, you can also insert new people or backgrounds into photos and add special effects such as halos.

You could take a picture of your spouse showing off his childhood coonskin cap that he just rediscovered in the attic, and within minutes e-mail the shot to your grandson. Or if his parents have a digital camera, you could be looking at a picture of him happily showing off the new gap in his smile from losing his first tooth moments earlier.

Most such digital cameras have a video-out port, so you can show your snapshots on your TV or record them on your VCR. You can load them into your personal computer, print them out, post them on a Web page, or e-mail them to family virtually anywhere.

Many family members store the images in a secure, password-protected photo album at one of the many online photo sharing services that offer free membership. After you upload the pictures to your own personal online album, friends and family can view them and order copies directly from the service which will print and mail them.

Videophone Systems

Regardless of how far away you live from your grandchild, you can still see him as often as you want by using the latest in video technology. Obviously, nothing beats being there. But seeing live pictures of him while talking to him from the comfort of your home can be the next best thing.

Some videophones hook up just like an answering machine and plug into any analog phone line between your regular phone and the wall jack. Once it's hooked up, you're good to go—as long as the person on the other end of the line has a compatible videophone device. Within a few seconds both parties see a live, full-color video feed. You don't need a computer or pay any extra fees or sign a contract.

Another kind of videophone uses your television to see your caller. Because it is a stand-alone device, you don't need a computer to video-conference over the Internet. Connect a standard telephone and a television to the videophone, plug in a standard Ethernet network cable connected to your broadband Internet connection, and you are ready to enjoy real-time video, at up to 30 frames per second, with your grandchild, assuming his family has the device as well.

In early 2004, the cost of videophones averaged between $200 and $300 apiece.

> **Parent from Portland, Oregon, on the Net:** *"I purchased [a videophone] so that distant grandparents in New York can see their new granddaughter. It is extremely easy to use and my computer-illiterate parents had no trouble getting this hooked up. This . . . concept is amazing and it makes my parents feel so much better when they can see their kids and grandkids three thousand miles away on the videophone versus just a phone call."*

A less expensive option is the webcam or PC camera for one-on-one video chatting with your grandchild. The camera, about the size of a computer mouse, can be mounted on your home PC or Mac monitor or even a notebook and comes with a software package. With the click of a button you can send fast, clear voice and video mail to your family easily. Some cameras have an integrated microphone, so users can simply plug it in and begin video-talking with their grandchildren. PC cameras and webcams can cost between $25 and $150.

> **Delores (Mom-mom) Lee, on *Good Morning America*:** *"I communicate with my four grandchildren over the Internet. My kids live in Queens and I live in Delaware, so we don't get to see*

*them a lot except holidays and special occasions. My son has a
camera hooked up to the computer so when we talk to each other
over the Internet, we can see them and interact with them."*

Camcorders

Who needs Blockbuster? Make your own videos and DVDs—and get everyone in the family involved. Designate someone in each household to be the family video director and have fun exchanging homemade videos and DVDs.

If you can afford it, buy your adult child a camcorder for the holidays. Then harp on him or her to send you videos of your grandkid. If you don't have a video camera, rent one or borrow one and insist the parents obtain one too.

Make at least one tape solely for your grandchild. Don't stand in front of the camcorder as if you were a graduate of the Ed Sullivan School of Emcees. Loosen up. Sing a song, act goofy like a *Laugh-In* alumni, tell a quick story, wrestle with the dog, sing like a Parrot Head. You're trying to connect with your grandchild. Depending on his age, keep your video segment short and sweet because his attention span will last about as long as it took Bullwinkle to get into trouble. Speak directly to him just as if he was there in person. But remember: Keep it brief.

Encourage your adult children to make the filming of your grandchild a fun experience for him. It doesn't have to be a Spielberg production. The best shots are those darling moments when he's performing or learning to swim or having fun at a petting zoo.

Share these videos with other family members. Family video exchanges help grandchildren grasp the concept of the extended family, of aunts and uncles and cousins. It's a way of keeping everyone connected.

Long-distance grandparents Vic and Lucille Twomey of Roseville, Illinois, have grandchildren in Oregon and Wisconsin. They all stay in touch through a traveling family video. A tape of the grandkids in Oregon is sent to the Wisconsin branch of the family. Members there view the tape and then add their own shots before sending it on to Vic and Lucille in Illinois. After enjoying the video of all their grandkids, the grandparents shoot their segment and ship the tape back to the Oregon family. When the tape is full, the family starts a fresh one. That way, everyone gets to see how the little ones and all the other relatives change and grow.

> **Tom (Grandpa) Andersen:** *"My granddaughter Sara is three and she knows how to run the VCR, so she loves getting videos from us. We live on opposite coasts, so videos are the best way to watch her grow. We miss being there with her, but at least the videos give both of us a chance to stay in closer touch than just the telephone."*

If you want to spend the bucks on the new parents, buy them a DVD camcorder for taking candid shots of your grandchild. The camcorder produces DVD recordings that can be played back in most current PC and home DVD players. The disc-based recording system allows for quick access to favorite scenes and pictures without the fuss of rewinding and fast-forwarding. You have the flexibility to do some simple in-camera editing as well as design a playlist of video clips and rearrange the order of the scenes and images without modifying the video. You can also shoot still images for viewing on either a PC or TV.

Camera Phones

You can send instant images to your grandchild or receive instant pictures of him with camera phones. The latest generation of cell phones feature models that are integrated with still cameras, some that even have video capability. With multimedia message service, you can use your cell phone to send still images, movie clips, and sounds along with words—all in one message.

So if you are in Strawberry Fields, you can send an instant postcard directly to family members with compatible phones. You can also send a link to the photos by e-mail to anyone with an e-mail address and, with a text message, explain where to view the pictures over the Internet, such as an online photo sharing service.

The days of carrying photos of your grandchildren in a wallet may soon be over, because you can store pictures of them in a personal and portable photo album in your camera phone.

Photos can be uploaded to your own personal Web site where they can be seen by others using a PC or Web-enabled cell phone. This "moblogging," or mobile weblogging, lets you use your cell phone to instantly share photographs, text, audio, and even video. If the parents have that capability, they can send pictures of your grandchild's first haircut right to your cell phone no matter where you are (as long as you have the proper service).

> **Megan Morrone:** *"With all the technology out today, I still wish my parents lived closer. Yes, they can see pictures of [her daughter] Annabella and see how she's changed because of the Internet, but there are some things technology can't do. They can't hold her and play with her and baby-sit."*

Telephone

Despite all the high-tech gadgets, Alexander Graham Bell's invention is still a long-distance grandparents' best friend. So use it!

If money is a problem for your grandchild's parents, give them pre-paid phone cards. If you can afford it, get an 800 number so that they'll call you more often. In many cases, the toll-free number doesn't cost anything to set up and doesn't require a new line. However, the cost per minute is likely to be higher (as much as double) than the rate of a long-distance call that you initiate. Using an Internet-based phone service can cut your callings costs too. At least your grandchild's parents can't raise expense as an issue for not calling frequently. (Of course, you don't have to wait for them to call. You can pick up the phone, too.)

> **Alisa (Nana) Dollar:** *"We had just come home and there was a message on the answering machine. Our granddaughter was singing her rendition of 'Twinkle, Twinkle, Little Star.' For Nana and*

Pop not being around her but three or four times a year, that brought happy tears to our eyes. Little things like that really do mean a lot."

Susan Newman suggests you plan your calls rather than pick up the phone at your convenience. Know your grandchild's routine, preschool hours, naps, meals, and bedtime. Then call at an appropriate time. If you phone at the wrong time, you could face an unsatisfying, hurried conversation.

It doesn't matter how young your grandchild is, it's important for both of you to communicate.

Elly (Granny) Shodell: *"When our grandson Andy was just a baby, we called him regularly and always made animal noises so he would have an audio recognition of us along with the photographs that my son showed him. That helped a lot to keep a connection with him between our visits."*

"You should be knowledgeable about what your grandchild is interested in," says Newman. "What's going on in his playgroup or in preschool? Who are his best friends? You might need to talk to the parents first to find out things about him. Then you can have a fulfilling conversation that relates to him. You'll be able to ask the right questions to get more than a one-word answer.

"You can always find time to call your grandchild. Pick up the phone while you're cooling down from your workout and talk to him or use the cell phone during your commute home. Most young children don't talk on the phone for very long so you should make the most of it."

Fax Machines and Scanners

If you have access to a fax machine, use it to brighten your grandchild's day. Fax a picture, riddle, or comic strip you think he might like. Or fax him a silly drawing and a sweet note just for him. Urge his parents to fax you things that he drew.

Scanners allow you to do virtually anything a fax can do, only better. They can duplicate a color photo, drawing, or text into your computer, allowing you to then post the document or graphic on a Web page or e-mail it to your grandchild.

Snail Mail

Children love to receive mail. So send your grandchild notes, postcards, letters, and little gifts on a regular basis.

If you're on the road a lot, pick up a postcard of each place you visit, jot a note about how much you miss him and are thinking about him, and send it off. Traveling grandparents often send their grandchildren an album or a special box for the kids to store their collection of postcards.

"You don't have to go anywhere to keep your grandchild 'in mail,'" says Newman. "Send a postcard from a local restaurant, art gallery, or hotel."

> **Kate (Grandma) Williamson:** *"My job requires much traveling. When I'm on the road, I gather the free boxed soaps and shampoos from my hotel rooms and send them to my granddaughter."*

"Grandchildren will look at postcards over and over when they're little," says Newman. "When the children grow up, those cards will have much more meaning to them because it's proof that you've cared about them from the time they were toddlers."

Don't expect to get a written response after every letter or postcard you send. Do it for the joy it brings your grandchild. However, you can boost your chances of receiving return mail by sending him a package of self-addressed stamped envelopes. It makes it easy on his parents to encourage him to respond. If he's a preschooler, ask him to send you a drawing for you to put on the refrigerator or on the wall where you work.

Send him a stack of prestamped postcards that the post office sells and have him draw you a picture every week. If he's learning to read, keep a stack of the cards for yourself so that you can quickly send him an endearing note. Make sure to print in large bold letters.

Have a unique signature or picture on the back of every envelope you send him—a smiley face, a rubber stamp or wax impression, or anything that means you and you alone. Take a cue from a grandma who uses only purple ink when she writes to her grandchildren or a grandpa who uses only green envelopes in mail to his grandson. Even if your grandchild can't read, he can recognize something special from Nana or Papa.

> **Randee (Grammy) Peters:** *"As a long-distance grandmother, I must share my grandson with three other grandmothers, so I try to make him aware of me by using his sense of smell. Joshua is still too young to read so what I do is scent my letters and postcards to him with my perfume. It's the same perfume I wear whenever I see him. That way, he can equate the scent with me."*

Try to find the time to actually pen a letter. Even if he has trouble reading it, his parents can read it to him. For a nice touch, include in the envelope a little present such as stickers, candy, magnets, a dried flower, trading cards, or even a dollar or two for him to spend.

It really doesn't take much effort to send your grandkid a little gift simply because you love him. Whenever you're at the grocery store or drugstore picking up things for yourself, take a few extra seconds to find something he would enjoy, whether it's a Barney pencil or a Rugrats deck of cards.

> **Nana Lana:** *"I like to surprise my two grandkids, Sammy and Mandy, by sending them little gifts like stickers, money, and books for no reason other than to let them know I'm thinking about them."*

> **David (Pop-Pop) Pilgrim:** *"I'm a glassblower and I don't get to see my kids or grandkids as much as I'd like because we're so far away from each other. On holidays, I make everyone a special figure or ornament. No two are alike. I do the same for their birthdays. It's my way of trying to be there."*

Newman suggests that if your company or volunteer organization has hats, mugs, T-shirts, or other items with the group's logo, send them to your grandchild. It's more than just a reminder that you're thinking about him; it's a way for him to connect with who you are in the work world and what social issues are important to you.

No matter how busy you are, it's well worth the extra time to correspond with your grandchild. The feeling you get when you receive a drawing or note that he made especially for Nana and Papa is second to none. Not only that but you're nurturing the love of writing and reading—and the love between a grandparent and a grandchild.

If you're real busy, ship special treats to your grandchild on a regular basis. Mail-order houses will send most anything from candies to cookies to flavored popcorn. Many houses will include a brief message from you too.

Long-distance grandparents are discovering literary ways to connect with their grandchildren through magazines, book clubs, and newsletters. Consider gifting your grandkid with a subscription to an age-appropriate magazine such as *Humpty Dumpty* (for ages four to six) or *Turtle* (for ages two to five). Every time he receives the magazine, it will remind him of you. You might want to sign up for two subscriptions to the same magazine—one for him and one for you. That way, you can discuss the magazine on a regular basis. Common interests are built, and it is an excellent way to see what he enjoys most.

If you're at the bookstore, spend a few extra minutes to pick up a book for him. Inscribe it, and send it to him.

Sign up for a children's book club that will send him monthly selections. But read the fine print of the club's agreement. Some clubs offer a fixed number of books, others choose the books for you, and several won't let you cancel unless you've paid for a certain amount of books.

> **Harry (Papa) Yeatts:** *"We joined a kid's book club in our granddaughter's name. Once a month or so, she receives a book that we've selected. Her parents always tell her that the new book in the mail came from Nana and Papa. The books let her know we're thinking of her."*

If your grandchild is nearing school age and has a special interest such as whales, tigers, or birds, join a wildlife organization together.

Choose one that offers a colorful, graphically-pleasing newsletter or publication. It will give you two something to talk about. Or participate in an adopt-an-animal program offered by many zoos and organizations, which also provide newsletters or updates on the animals.

Kirk Leiter: *"I swear I'm on the mailing list of every wildlife organization in America. Many of their pitch letters include stamps, stickers, and cards, so I collect them and pass them on to my grandkids. They love it."*

Photos

Get your puss in front of your grandchild as many times as possible. You want more than your fifteen minutes of fame in his eyes. So be shameless. Put your photo on buttons, magnets, mouse pads, coffee cups, T-shirts, sweatshirts, and aprons for him or his parents to use. You can find computer-photo or video-photo services that offer these products in most malls.

Insert your photo in a toy or holiday ornament specially designed to hold a picture and send it to him. Such items are for sale in many gift catalogs.

Get in the habit of taking photos of yourself doing whatever it is you do—soaking in your hot tub, cross-country skiing, tinkering with your '65 Mustang. Send these photos to your grandchild. In fact, keep a steady stream going. Let him see what an interesting person you are. (You might not want to send pictures of you at the come-dressed-as-your-favorite-*Rocky-Horror-Picture-Show*-character party.) Put captions on all the photos because they can provide an early reading experience.

Many experts say that as elders, it's our responsibility to send grandchildren photos of us from the past, so they can get a sense of family history. Oh, sure. Can't you just see sending the little one pictures of Papa with his long, stringy hair and scraggly beard hauled off by police at a protest rally? Or of Nana go-go dancing in her skimpy tube top, hot pants, and shiny white boots? But on the off chance that you can rustle up some not-too-embarrassing snapshots from the past, mail them to him.

Have an informal picture taken of you, put it in a frame, and send it off. Ask his parents not only to display it in a high-traffic area of the house but also to point to it often and refer to you by name. (To ensure the parents' cooperation, threaten to mail your grandson the photo of his mom when she was being potty-trained.) Pick a talking picture frame. A recording unit attached to the frame lets you record a message in your own voice. Each time your grandchild presses the button on the frame, he will hear you.

Make sure all family members, including your grandchild, have a photograph of you to carry around and show others, the way you do with theirs.

Each time you visit your grandchild or he visits you, take plenty of pictures of you two together. Put the photos in a little album as a reminder of the great time you both had.

Photography is a two-way street. Badger the parents into taking photos of your grandchild on a regular basis. If the parents have a film camera, buy film for them or have them send the undeveloped film to you; heck, buy them a disposable camera. Impress upon them the importance and joy to you of seeing him growing up. If your grandchild is old enough, send him a disposable camera and tell him to take pictures of whatever he wants. Make it easy on everyone by including the return mailer and the money to have the film developed.

Jane (Nana) Trebble: *"We have a tradition of having each family take their own photo at least once a year. Everyone has to be in the same position from year to year so we can all compare the changes over time."*

Voice Recorders

To connect with your long-distance infant grandchild, record your favorite nursery rhymes, lullabies, Motown hits, or sorority songs (the cleaned-up versions), and send them to your grandchild's parents to play on their microcassette or cassette recorder. Let your voice become familiar to the baby. When you finally see him, he'll recognize your voice.

Once your grandchild is old enough to carry on a conversation, start an ongoing taped dialogue with him. While you're battling rush hour traffic, keep a tape recorder next to you and record jokes, silly thoughts, old protest songs, a story, whatever you think he'll enjoy. Send it to him with the understanding that he'll record something and return it to you. (Include a self-addressed, stamped mailer.) It probably will be a short reply, but a cherished one. When that tape is filled, save it and start a new one. Your long-distance correspondence can keep going for years—and they will become priceless mementos.

"If your grandchild is in a recital, ask his parents to record it and mail it to you," says Newman. "The tape will allow you to enjoy your grandchild's performance as many times as you like."

You don't have to use a tape recorder. For under $100, you can get a digital voice recorder and e-mail your voice messages to him. If his parents have one, they can record his voice and send it directly to your PC.

Joy (Grammy) Tucker: *"About every other month I record a storybook on tape and then send it, along with the book, to my grandkids. They follow along as Grammy reads it to them. I blow a whistle every time they are supposed to turn the page."*

Internet Bargain Trips

You might be able to see your long-distance grandchild more often than you think—if you're flexible and can take off for a long weekend. It's quite affordable. But there are some catches: you need to live within an easy commute to a major airport to make it worthwhile, and you can't go whenever you want. And, oh yes, you must be online.

More than a dozen airlines and online travel services offer last-minute, Internet-only fares to selected destinations at discounts of up to 75 percent off regular coach. In most cases, available flights are announced on Wednesday night for Saturday departures, returning the next Monday or Tuesday. The airlines will post these specials on their

Web sites and some will even e-mail the flight information to subscribers who sign up for this free service.

Airlines use cyberspace to dump unsold seats a few days before departure. For example, each Wednesday, US Airways tantalizes us with low weekend airfares out of Charlotte, North Carolina—the closest big-city airport to our home. (For a January, 2004, weekend, we could fly to Dallas, Chicago, or Tampa for $158 round-trip.) But the destinations change every week. You have to pounce on the bargain when the flight is heading to a city near your grandchild. Many times these flights are sold out within a day of being posted on the Net.

Often, airlines will engage in secret price wars, cutting fares for a few hours or a day on competitive routes. To find these bargain fares before they vaporize, go to www.air-fare.com, which posts fares every weekday morning, and www.bestfares.com, which updates new fares throughout the day. For other last-minute bargains, check out www.expedia.com and www.travelocity.com.

Be spontaneous. You don't always have to get together only for holidays and special occasions. Take off just because you want to spend time with your grandchild and his parents. And if your spouse can't break away from work, go by yourself.

> **Randee (Grammy) Peters:** *"My business trips sometimes take me through Chicago. When that happens, I try to schedule a layover for a day so I can see [her grandson] Joshua. He lives only thirty minutes from the airport. Once I had a three-hour layover and got a chance to see him because his mom brought him to the airport. It made my week."*

Vacations Together

Grandparents are hitting the road with their grandkids in record numbers. Twenty percent of grandparents have been on a trip with their grandchildren in the past year, according to *American Demographics*. "Grandtravel," as it is referred to in the industry, represented more than a quarter of all trips taken with children in 2003, says the Travel

Industry Association of America. Boomers already constitute almost half of the total family travel market and spend more on their family vacations than any other group.

And it's likely to continue growing. An overwhelming majority (78 percent) of kids ages six to eight say they "would really like to" vacation with their grandparents, according to a recent survey by the travel marketing firm Yesawich, Pepperdine, and Brown. The survey revealed that about one in three grandparents has traveled with grandkids in the past twelve months.

"To reconnect and to reaffirm their vital connection, grandparents and grandchildren need a place where they can be alone together and share time all their own away from the demands of their everyday lives," says Dr. Kornhaber. "They have a wonderful time."

To help bridge the distance gap, Dr. Kornhaber and his wife Carol started the Grandparent-Grandchild summer camp at the Sagamore Conference Center (the former Vanderbilt estate) near Raquette, New York, in the Adirondack Mountains in 1985. Here, grandparents and grandchildren spend time together playing games, doing crafts, enjoying nature, and just having fun. There are no TVs or private phones in the rustic lodge settings—and, most importantly, no parents either. The camp is now operated under the auspices of the Sagamore Foundation and ElderHostel. (For further information, see Grandparent-Grandchild Travel in the appendix.)

> **Holly (Grandma) Noble, of California, speaking about attending the camp with her granddaughter Hannah of Vermont:** *"She'll always remember the summer she went to camp with Grandma."*

Many churches are offering faith-based summer camp outings for grandparents and grandchildren. The Grandkidsandme Foundation (www.grandkidsandme.com) sponsors camps at various times of the year in Wisconsin and Minnesota.

Several nonprofit organizations offer intergenerational trips that combine learning with sightseeing, field trips, and recreation. These trips, with varying age requirements for grandchildren, range from hiking in the mountains to visiting rain forests; from beachcombing in the Caribbean to exploring European castles and caves. Among those organizations offering such grandparent-grandchild trips are the Sierra Club (www.sierraclub.org), ElderHostel (www.elderhostel.org), and the University of New Hampshire's Familyhostel Learning Vacations (www.learn.unh.edu/familyhostel).

If you can afford it, why not splurge with a once-in-a-lifetime multigenerational vacation? Go somewhere fascinating together. To learn about special deals for grandparent-grandchildren trips, talk to your travel agent or check out grandparenting Web sites that often highlight such vacations.

Today there are tour companies that specialize in intergenerational vacations. Mostly their tours are in the summer, when youngsters are out of school. They can schedule anything from trips to Washington, D.C., to a safari in Kenya. Some have age minimums. Among the companies that specialize in family trips are AFC Tours (www.afc-tours.com) and Rascals in Paradise (www.rascalsinparadise.com).

Some countries are trying to tap into grandtravel by arranging trips that tie in with favorite kids' films. For example, the British Tourism Authority has printed 500,000 maps to guide fans to the castles and cathedrals that were stand-ins for haunts in the Harry Potter movies. The Lord of the Ring trilogy has spurred tours to New Zealand.

If you have money to burn, try one of the pricey national or international tours arranged by Grandtravel, which follows an itinerary developed by a team of teachers, psychologists, and leisure counselors.

"You already know how valuable travel can be to a grandchild, how it can light a fire in their active imagination in unexpected ways, and deliver a lifetime of payoffs," says Helena T. Koenig, grandmother and founder of Grandtravel. "A love of buildings might be developed at the Colosseum in Rome; a delight in marine biology might begin while snorkeling at the Great Barrier Reef; or a historian might be born while standing in the Tower of London. Now, more than ever, appreciating new cultures is vitally important for our grandchildren. Anyone can leave their grandchildren money, but these grandparents want to leave them with memories. They want to participate in making these children's lives with them significant."

Cruises are becoming an increasingly popular, cost-effective way for grandparents to spend vacation time with the grandchildren. Most of the major cruise lines such as Carnival, Celebrity, Disney, Holland American, Norwegian, and Princess have programs geared for children as young as two with activities and counselors for different age groups. But there are still plenty of activities for the generations to do together. The ships offer bigger staterooms to accommodate larger families or have adjoining rooms.

Hotels are wooing grandparents with discounts and freebies for the grandkids such as a disposable camera, popcorn, and free use of the hotel's videos and games. All-inclusive resorts often have dollar-stretching programs that entice grandparents to bring the grandkids. Call any of the hotel chains' reservation numbers and ask if or what grandparent programs they are offering.

In many cases, money is the biggest factor in preventing grandparents from visiting their grandchildren.

"The family must decide to give a high priority to having grandparents and grandchildren spend as much time as possible together," says Dr. Kornhaber. "This means that the financial resources of the family must be pooled to make this happen. Establish a family policy that recognizes the reality of distance and makes a commitment to try to be as close as possible. If the grandparents can't come to the grandchildren, then send the grandchildren—when they're old enough—to Grandma and Grandpa."

Grandparents' Legal Issues

Powers of Attorney

WHEN WE BOOMERS WERE KIDS and our parents wanted a break from us, they usually shipped us off to Grandma's house or had Grandma come over to baby-sit while they hopped in their Ford Fairlane and drove on the new interstate to Niagara Falls or Mount Rushmore. Grandma was now in charge, and no one outside the family questioned her authority. She didn't need, nor have, anything in writing to say she was the boss while the parents were away.

Don't try that today, please. As a devoted grandparent, you need to be legally prepared to care for your grandchild or else you could face serious problems concerning your responsibility for, and relationship with, your grandchild.

If you're baby-sitting for him while his parents are snowboarding in Keystone for the week or if you regularly care for him, you should have legal authorization to make critical decisions on his behalf, especially in case of a medical emergency. Without it, your grandchild may not get the swift care he deserves.

Because of strict rules and regulations affecting health care today, grandparents need this document. According to the Grandparents Rights Organization, "other than in life-threatening situations, many doctors and hospitals will refuse a grandparent (or other third party) to secure medical treatment for a minor child unless the adult has a guardianship order from a court or a medical authorization form signed by a parent."

In most cases, you don't have to go to court or even visit an attorney. A simple power of attorney (such as one of the three samples shown in this chapter) signed by the parents will give you the proper authorization. Most states also require that such a form be witnessed and notarized.

The following information on powers of attorney was adapted with permission from the Genesee County (Michigan) Strong Families/Safe Children's Grandparent Guidebook.

The power of attorney form can be as broad or as specific as the parents wish. For example, it can give you decision-making power just for medical situations. It can also be all-encompassing, granting you the legal right to do things that the parents would do on behalf of your grandchild.

This authorization is good to use if:

- the child's parents are willing and available to sign the forms

- you need to make decisions for the child

- you need this power for more than a short time

- the child's parents want to be able to take back the power quickly at a later time

- you want the parents to spell out the specific powers and decision-making abilities that they are granting you

- you don't want the court involved

Depending on the state, a parental power of attorney is good for only a certain length of time, such as six months or a year. If you and the parents want it to be for a shorter time, you should say so on the form. For a longer period of time, the parents will have to fill out another power of attorney when the previous one expires.

The power of attorney can be changed or taken away at any time by the parents by signing another document saying they revoke the powers they had given you.

If you're baby-sitting for a specific period of time or watch your grandchild regularly, it's wise to have a special power of attorney for medical care. Here is a sample:

SPECIAL POWER OF ATTORNEY FOR MEDICAL CARE

We/I, _____ , hereby name _____ as
name of parent(s)   your name and/or your spouse's

our/my attorney in fact (hereinafter "our/my agent"), and grant
to our/my agent the limited authority to care for our/my child,
_____ , as follows:
name of child

1. We/I grant to our/my agent the authority to consent to all
   medical care necessary to our/my child's health and well-
   being during the time our/my child is in the care of our/my
   agent.

2. This power includes, and is expressly limited to, the following: the power to consent to all medical, dental, and/or hospital care, treatment, and procedures.

3. [If there are more specific purposes for allowing the power,
   write it here: _____ .]

4. The provisions in this document are to be construed with
   this express purpose in mind.

This power shall expire and all authority thereunder is revoked

on _____ .
    date of expiration

Date: _____

Signature(s) of Parent(s) _____ .

Print/Type Name(s) & Address:

_____

_____

_____

Phone: _____

(continued)

On _____ , _____ , who
　　　　　　　date　　　　　　　　　　*name of parent(s)*
are/is known by me, appeared before me to execute this document, and have/has acknowledged this to be their/his/her free
act and deed.

_____ Notary Public, _____ County,

My Commission Expires: _____

Signature of Witness _____

Signature of Witness _____

A general power of attorney is the same kind of permission, but it gives you, as the grandparent, the right to do almost anything a parent could do concerning the child's health, support, care, and well-being. (It does not grant standing in a custody suit.) Here is a sample:

GENERAL POWER OF ATTORNEY
CONSENT FOR CARE OF MY CHILD

We/I, _____ , hereby name _____
　　　　name of parent(s)　　　　　　　　　*your name and/or your spouse's*
as our/my attorney in fact (hereinafter "our/my agent"), and grant to our/my agent the authority to care for our/my child,
_____ , as follows:
　child's name

1. It is understood that _____ shall remain in
　　　　　　　　　　　　　　child's name
   the care of our/my agent until _____ .
　　　　　　　　　　　　　　　　date of termination

2. We/I grant to our/my agent the power and authority to do all things necessary to ensure the safety and well-being of our/my child while in the care of our/my agent. This power includes [cross out and initial or delete any that do not

apply] the power to consent to all medical, psychological, dental, and/or hospital care, treatment, and procedures; consent to receive, deliver, or pay money and property due to our/my child; receipt of all confidential information or records concerning our/my child; enrollment of our/my child in any school, place of worship, club, etc. This delegation does not include the power to consent to adoption of this child.

3. The express purpose of this power is to allow the agent to do all things necessary to ensure the safe and efficient care of our/my child, and to do all things necessary for his/her care.

4. [*If there are further specific purposes, write them here*]

_____

5. All provisions contained herein are to be interpreted with this/those express purpose(s) in mind.

This power shall expire and all authority thereunder is revoked on _____ .
  date of expiration

Date: _____

Signature(s) of parent(s) _____ .

Print/Type Name(s) & Address:

_____

_____

_____

Phone: _____

(continued)

On _____ , _____ , who
  date   *name of parent(s)*
are/is known by me, appeared before me to execute this document, and have/has acknowledged this to be their/his/her free
act and deed.

_____ Notary Public, _____ County,

My Commission Expires: _____

Signature of Witness _____

Signature of Witness _____

In cases when you're involved in long-term care for your grandchild, you might need written authorization from the parents to deal
with school issues involving him, from teacher conferences to field
trips.

Many agencies and offices have a legal duty to keep information
about children private. They are not allowed to release information to
anyone other than a parent, unless the parent signs a paper saying this
is okay. This is an important protection for children, but it may keep
you from talking to your grandkid's teachers or seeing his school
records.

You can have access to this education-related information for as
long as the parental authorization form allows, or until the parent
takes away your permission. Here is a sample:

RELEASE OF EDUCATION-RELATED INFORMATION

We/I _____ hereby authorize the release of all infor-
  name of parent(s)
mation, confidential and otherwise, written or verbal, pertaining
to our/my child, _____ , to _____ .
  name of child   *your name and/or your spouse's*
We/I authorize _____ to request and receive
  your name and/or your spouse's

any and all information from any school, teacher, education administrator, scholastic or educational records, or any other educational source regarding our/my child's schooling, education, educational behavior, grades, homework, schoolwork, learning ability or disabilities, psychological or emotional treatment or development, and all information related to schooling or education whether or not subject to heightened privacy standards. This release includes [*cross out and initial or delete the items that don't apply*] permission to attend and participate in school activities for or with our/my child, such as field trips, parent-teacher conferences, parents' school associations of any kind, and the like. We/I release all agencies, schools, educational institutions, boards, teachers, administrators, persons, offices, and the like from any liability on account of any disclosure authorized by this release. A photocopy of this release shall be acceptable as an original. This release shall expire on _____ or

<small>date of expiration</small>

upon our/my written revocation, whichever is sooner.

Date: _____

Signature(s) of parent(s) _____ .

Print/Type Name(s) & Address:

_____

_____

_____

Phone: _____

Child's Date of Birth/Social Security # _____

(*continued*)

On _____, _____, who
　　　　　date　　　　　　　　　*name of parent(s)*
are/is known by me, appeared before me to execute this document, and have/has acknowledged this to be their/his/her free
act and deed.

_____ Notary Public, _____ County,

My Commission Expires: _____

Signature of Witness _____

Signature of Witness _____

With all of these cases, keep the completed original form in a safe place. But first make copies and use them whenever possible. If there is more than one child involved, all their names can go on the same power of attorney form or you can use a separate form for each child. If you and your spouse are going to be agents, both your names must be on the form.

These forms must be signed by all custodial parents or guardians. If more than one person has physical and legal custody, they all must sign. In most states, the parents must sign in front of a notary public. If both parents will not be able to sign in front of the same notary at the same time, you should get a separate power of attorney from each custodial parent. Because laws differ from state to state, it's best to contact your personal lawyer if you have any questions concerning powers of attorney.

Grandparent Visitation Rights

It's sad, but an increasing number of grandparents are relying on mediators or waging court battles simply for the right to spend time with their own grandchildren. For them, multigenerational family harmony is something that could only be experienced on old reruns of *The Waltons*.

Most such visitation disputes occur when the grandparents' former son-in-law or daughter-in-law has custody of the children after a bitter divorce or the tragic death of a parent. For whatever reason, the custodial parent denies the grandparents access to the grandchildren. Fortunately, state laws provide grandparents the opportunity to seek reasonable visitation rights.

Although no one knows how many such court cases are filed in the United States today, noted grandparents' rights advocate Richard Victor says the number of cases his law firm handles has increased tenfold since 1978. Because of the enormity of the problem, he founded the nonprofit Grandparents Rights Organization (GRO). It advocates laws that protect the grandparent-grandchild relationship and provides information to grandparents, legislators, and media and assists support groups.

Says Victor, GRO executive director and an attorney in Bloomfield Hills, Michigan, "When I got involved in this issue in 1978, there were no laws [concerning grandparents' rights]. It wasn't because the legislators thought grandparents shouldn't have rights; it was because nobody thought such laws were necessary. Well, they were. We helped get laws passed in all fifty states."

However, the legal rights of grandparents differ widely from one state to another, and efforts to establish a uniform law that applies nationwide have failed so far. To make matters more confusing, many states are rewriting their laws concerning grandparents' visitation in light of the U.S. Supreme Court ruling in 2000.

In a plurality opinion delivered by Justice Sandra Day O'Connor (herself a grandmother), the court held in *Troxel v. Granville* that the state of Washington's statute that allowed anybody to obtain visitation as long as it was in the child's best interest was unconstitutional. The ruling came in a case in which Jenifer and Gary Troxel objected to having their visits with their grandchildren Isabelle and Natalie Granville cut by the kids' mother Tommie to once a month after the death of the Troxels' son Brad, the children's unmarried father. The 6–3 opinion asserted that courts can't force custodial parents into allowing visitation rights to "third parties"—a category that grandparents are lumped into, along with other in-laws, significant others, friends, associates, and even stepfamilies.

"There is a presumption that fit parents act in the best interests of their children," Justice O'Connor wrote in the majority opinion. "The Fourteenth Amendment protects the fundamental rights of parents to make decisions concerning the care, custody, and control of their children."

However, a court may intervene if it can be shown the child would be substantially harmed, or potentially harmed, by not seeing the third party in question. Furthermore, the court listed with favor some examples of grandparent visitation statutes that accord adequate weight to the parent's viewpoint and others that permit an award of visitation only when visitation has been completely or unreasonably denied. Thus, the court suggested that more narrowly-drawn grandparent visitation statutes do not violate the Constitution.

"The media depicted the Troxel case as one in which grandparents lost the right to visit their grandchildren, but that's not what the Supreme Court said," Victor explains. "The court didn't say the grandparenting laws in all fifty states were unconstitutional. It said the Washington law—which wasn't even a grandparenting law—was too broad.

"The people against grandparent relationships were asking the court to throw out all laws to make it very difficult if not impossible for grandparents to ever get visitation, and the court wouldn't do that. To me that was a victory. The Supreme Court did a good job. Unfortunately, the media misunderstood it, and so did many state legislators and judges."

As a result, each state is handling the matter in its own way. Some are reluctant to act while others are redrafting their laws; some are reaffirming grandparents' rights while others are making visitation more difficult. Not only that, each state has slightly different interpretations and standards on which their courts base their decisions.

To pass constitutional muster, every state law concerning grandparents' visitation must provide a presumption that fit parents act in the best interest of the grandchild. The law must also give special weight to the parents' decision and place the burden of proof on the grandparents that visitation is in the grandchild's best interest.

"Whenever there has been a death or a divorce, the custodial parent or surviving parent who is raising the child is no longer legally related to the former in-laws, but those in-laws—the grandparents—are still related to the child," says Victor. "So advocates for grandparents and grandchildren are asking the state laws to recognize the family of the child and define family through the child's eyes and not the adults' eyes. Each state will make the determination as to what requirements need to be shown in order for grandparents to prevail.

"Imagine the agony a child feels when his parents and grandparents—adults whom he loves—don't like each other. This agony is intensified when he finds himself the 'prize' to be won or lost in legal disputes. Parents need to remember this, and realize that their children have rights that should not be denied unless it is in their best interests to do so.

"Studies have shown that multigenerational contact between children and their grandparents—and even great-grandparents—provides a special unconditional love and nurturing which is healthy for children. If death takes a grandparent from a grandchild, that's a tragedy. But if family bickering and vindictiveness deny a child the love of a grandparent, that's a shame."

Marilyn Daniels, Ph.D., conducted one of the first-ever studies of the grandparents' rights issue for the GRO.

"The general tenor of the grandpa.rents' responses were of people who had been through a terrible ordeal," she says. "One grandmother described holding her granddaughter one and only one time—in the hospital, the day of her birth. Another was haunted by the memory of her grandchild's face. She said she was 'having a hard time forgetting her, although I've been told to forget her.'

"As I studied the survey responses, I was amazed by the apparent senselessness of the withholders' actions. In many cases, it seemed that parents withheld the children with little or no provocation. I can think of few other examples in the field of family problems in which one category of persons is free to inflict misery on another so effortlessly and without social sanction."

According to the study, there is no typical kind of grandparent or custodial parent whose personal characteristics lead to a visitation dispute. "It can happen to any grandparent," Dr. Daniel warns.

In disputes over grandparent access to children, 50 percent of the cases involve former daughters-in-law or former sons-in-law (sometimes in collusion with their new partners); 32 percent involve "intact" families where the grandchild's parents are married; 9 percent involve an out-of-wedlock birth; 7 percent involve the death of the grandparents' own son or daughter; and 2 percent involve the adoption or foster care of the grandchild. Of the parents who deny their children access to grandparents, an overwhelming 81 percent are women (most likely because of the higher incidence of divorced mothers gaining custody).

"I was startled to find that although most of the grandparents knew the whereabouts of their grandchildren, some seemed to know little about the withholding parent, and many knew little about the withholding parent's new spouse or live-in lover," says Dr. Daniels.

"Many grandparents didn't know such basic information as the person's religion, occupation, education, times married, or total number of children. It's no wonder that so many grandparents worry about the well-being of their grandchildren. They find it maddening to know so little about these people who are living with, influencing, and acting as parents to their grandchildren. These other adults who have access to the children are virtual strangers to the grandparents."

The GRO survey found that 42 percent of the grandparents thought the withholding parents acted entirely on their own. Of the 44 percent who thought the parents were swayed by others, nearly two-thirds identified "the other grandparents" as influencing the withholder.

Withholders often make visiting difficult or embarrassing for grandparents. "This is an attempt to discourage contact without actually forbidding it," says Dr. Daniels. "Many of the grandparents in the study reported on how uncomfortable they felt when they attempted to visit."

Deliberate misunderstandings about the timing of the grandparents' visits are common. "Grandparents were left waiting in their cars or on porches during times of appointed visits," she reports. "Some grandparents were not invited to sit down, even when they were allowed inside the withholder's house. Sadly, when visits were allowed, the parents often exerted some kind of negative pressure on the situation, making the children feel strange about being friendly toward their grandparents. In a number of cases, these awkward feelings were later used by the parents as evidence that the children 'didn't want to see,' or 'didn't really like,' or 'didn't really know' the grandparents."

Obviously, the best way to avoid such a heart-wrenching situation is to work at keeping a good relationship with your adult child and his or her spouse. The next best thing is to legally protect your right and your grandchild's right to see each other.

> **Gramma Kay:** *"When our son divorced, I was devastated. I thought I'd never see [her grandson] Trevor again. But I made a determined effort to be friendly with his ex-wife even though we never had a really good relationship. She understands that Trevor deserves to see his gramma."*

If your child is in the midst of a divorce, encourage him or her to add grandparent visitation rights in the decree. Divorcing parents can prevent later intergenerational conflict by including in their separation agreement a provision stating specifically that both sets of grandparents will have visitation rights.

If it's too late for that and visitation rights were not included in the decree, you can apply to whatever local court has appropriate jurisdiction and seek the right to visit with an unmarried minor child. In most states, if the custodial parent has remarried and the new spouse has adopted your grandchild, you still have a right to petition the court for visitation rights with him. Every case must be determined upon its own facts and circumstances.

Don't think that just because you are related to your grandchild by blood you deserve visitation rights. It doesn't work that way. You have a responsibility to show that you can be trusted implicitly with the child's care. Drug or alcohol dependency or a history of mental illness or criminal activity would be valid reasons to be denied visitation. So would proof that there was little effort to foster a relationship with the grandchild or that the relationship was superficial and contrived. Be ready to prove that you have made every effort to be a good grandparent. Keep records of attempts at communication.

You'll have a much tougher time arguing your case if both the mother and father in an intact family don't want you visiting, warns Victor. "There are challenges saying the constitutional rights of parents cannot be infringed by courts forcing them to grant grandparent visitation."

If your son or daughter is the noncustodial parent, try spending time with the grandchildren when they are visiting him or her. But don't bad-mouth the custodial parent to your grandchildren no matter how hard it is to keep your lips sealed. If the custodial parent feels he or she must "deprogram" the kids every time they come home from seeing you, the kids could end up brainwashed to dislike you or, more likely, they'll be barred from your life.

If the court had ruled for little visitation time or absolutely none for the parent, perhaps you need to work on helping your own adult child deal with whatever issues the court said exist that are preventing the parent from having custody, or even a normal amount of visitation time, with his or her children.

If you are denied access to your grandchildren for whatever reason, Victor offers these suggestions:

- Find alternative ways to continue the relationship. "Write letters and call. Let the grandchildren know you're part of their support network. And never, never make them feel they have an emotional conflict of interest. Even if you have to bite your tongue when you say something nice about the custodial parent, do it because you're doing it for the good of the children."
- Don't be too aggressive. If the custodial parent remarries, give him or her plenty of time to make the new marriage work. "Such family transitions are usually difficult for young children, who may be torn by loyalty to the divorced or deceased parent."
- Join or form a self-help support group in your area to exchange information, discuss problems, and promote local, state, and national laws.

- Before consulting an attorney, try to diffuse the situation by talking to the custodial parent. Call, write, or arrange a meeting with the parent to find out the motive for denying access to the grandchildren. "More often than not, visitation is not being denied because the parent thinks contact with the grandparents will be harmful for the children. Instead, the parent fears that the grandparents will talk to the children about him or her in an adverse way."

- Agree with the parent to recognize that the best interests of the children should be put first. "Make that the basis for the starting point of any communication."

- Offer to be a positive resource for baby-sitting, shopping, teaching, or mentoring.

- Avoid confrontational and accusatory statements. "You each have a right to think, feel, and believe in your own way."

- If necessary, use a third party such as a social worker, family counselor, or mediator. "Neutral mediators can help adults talk out and resolve family problems that brought about the breakup which resulted in the denial of access to the grandchildren. Reconciliation is preferable to litigation for everyone concerned—especially the children."

- If this informal mediation fails, consider litigation. "Turn to this as a last resort only if you feel it would be in the children's best interest."

- Spend time finding the right attorney. "Don't go out and find an attack dog or an attorney who, when he closes his file and gets paid, leaves nothing behind but scorched earth for the family. You need someone who cares, is willing to facilitate communication, specializes in family law, and has experience in third-party visitation rights. Often local bar associations will have listings for such attorneys through lawyer referral services."

- Present the attorney with documented evidence and lists of witnesses to support your contention that it's in the "best interest of the children"—the legal standard in most states—for them to see you. Your case is strengthened if you can show that a consistent, caring relationship existed between you and the children in the past.

Papa on the Net: *"For what we have been through to get to see our grandchildren, I wouldn't wish on anyone. The negative energy of battling in court—of dealing with lies, half-truths, and false accusations, not to mention legal fees—saps you of your inner strength. But was it worth it? Yes, because now we get to see our grandchildren."*

"There is an increase in the number of grandparents filing court actions because of divorce and unfortunate deaths of young parents with young children, leaving grandparents wanting to maintain a meaningful relationship with their grandchildren, their heritage," says Victor. "Also, many baby boomers are becoming grandparents, and they're not going to sit idly by and see their family amputated because their former son-in-law or daughter-in-law doesn't like them. So that's why there is an increase in court filings, although not necessarily in litigation."

Most states highly encourage mediation or alternative dispute resolution. "Ninety-seven percent of the cases are resolved without going to trial by specialists or good family law attorneys who sit the families down and get them talking," says Victor. "Never forget that the parents have a right to raise their children and the grandparents have a right to love those children. I always tell the families on both sides, 'You all have something in common.' And they look at me as if I'm crazy. I tell them, 'You love a child and the child loves you. So let's start from there.'"

Usually the issues aren't nearly as complicated as they appear to be, he says. Talking things out often leads to a simple solution. Victor cites an example from one of his cases in which he brokered an agreement between the mother and her child's grandmother:

Victor (to the mother): "Why won't you let Grandma see your child?"

Mother: "She takes my kid to fast-food restaurants."

Victor: "Grandma, do you do that?"

Grandmother: "Yes, there's nothing wrong with that. We like to do that and so does our grandchild."

Victor: "Well, you know what? Mom gets to decide what her child eats. If she will let you have visitation, would you agree not to take him to McDonald's or other fast-food places?"

Grandmother: "Well, yeah, if that's what I have to do, that's not a problem."

Victor (to the mother): "So if we have a court order that Grandma will lose her visitation if she takes your child to a fast-food place, will that satisfy you?"

Mother: "Yes."

Victor (to the mother): "Is there anything else that concerns you?"

Mother: "Well, no."

Case settled.

> **Nana on the Net:** *"If you care enough about your grandchildren, you'll fight to the death for them. If it means spending some of your profit-sharing, so be it."*

Because legislation varies from one state to another, even if you win your case, you will have to start all over again if your grandchild moves to another state. Among the court's criteria for a child's best interest:

- love, affection, and other emotional ties that exist between the child and grandparent
- the ability of the grandparent to provide the child proper care during visits
- the relationship between the grandparent and child prior to filing the petition
- the moral fitness of the grandparent
- the mental and physical health of the grandparent
- the reasonable preference of the child if the court deems him old enough
- any evidence that the grandparent tried to adversely affect the child's relationship with the parents
- any history of domestic violence or abuse involving the grandparent

Grandparent visitation rights are not intended or designed to supersede parental authority. But sometimes in desperate situations, it might be necessary to consider gaining custody of your grandchild. Consult an attorney and be ready to face a painful and emotional ordeal.

However, if you believe there is a threat to your grandchild's safety, experts advise that you must step in immediately to protect him. If there is evidence that he is being physically or emotionally abused, contact the department of social services in the state where he lives.

In extreme cases, some grandparents are reluctant to seek outside help for fear the parents will retaliate by barring them from visiting their grandchildren, says Dr. Arthur Kornhaber. "If little Harry's parents are smoking God-knows-what all day and Grandma wants to blow the whistle to the authorities, the parents can say, 'Call the cops, Grandma, and you'll never see Harry again.' However, the court could remove the child from the home in such a case, opening up other legal access for Grandma."

For those of you who must go through mediation or a court battle, hang tough and stay positive. Advises Dr. Kornhaber, "Keep your family as intact as possible, strive for healing, and never give up. Today, the Foundation for Grandparenting receives phone calls and letters from grandparents and grandchildren who have reunited and want to share their joy with others. Interestingly, many [custodial and once-adversarial] parents are also happy about this reunion. This confirms that people are capable of growing and changing for the better."

There's Enough to Go Around

Sharing Your Financial Assets

As a grandparent, perhaps you should think about sharing more than your love. If you haven't already, consider sharing some of your wealth. Sure, we boomers have been told that we're overextended and haven't stashed enough for retirement. Obviously, you have to take care of your own financial needs. But if circumstances allow, now is the time to help provide for your grandchildren's financial needs and future by giving them—and perhaps their parents—cash gifts, by establishing trusts, and/or by leaving them property.

Perhaps it's time to call a family conference to discuss the funding of your grandchildren's educational and recreational expenses. With costs continually rising, parents today might not have the resources to do this alone.

Maybe the young family needs your help paying for day care, preschool, medical bills, or gymnastic lessons. If you've got the dough, show them the money. Here's your chance to play John Beresford Tipton on a much more affordable—and meaningful—scale. You and your spouse each can give up to $11,000 a year tax-free to each grandchild (or to anyone else you wish, like your personal trainer or aromatherapist—but why waste it on them?).

According to the *Kiplinger Letter*, 52 percent of grandparents help pay for their grandchildren's education, 45 percent help pay for living expenses, and 25 percent help pay medical and dental costs.

Says Barbara Bowman of the Erikson Institute, "The conventional wisdom of a generation ago was that the kids should be able to make it on their own. Today young people are finding that it is not as easy to make it on their own as they had anticipated. It is important for grandparents to provide for some kind of resources.

"One issue is: 'If I give you money, you have to spend it my way.' That's not a very good way to support your adult children. If you can afford to give it, then give it. Assume your children will use it wisely or that they will use it for the specific purpose for which they need the money. To offer them money and tell them how to spend it deprives them of the opportunity to grow up."

Money can help take the pressure off them and make them better parents to your grandchildren, Bowman adds.

"Some grandparents give the money to the parents, believing the parents probably know what's best to do with it," says noted Certified Financial Planner Jeff Wallem, of Wallem Associates in Rockford, Illinois. "Often the parents are the ones who need the help. But then there's the issue of loss of control of your money. It depends on the relationship and trust you have with your adult children."

You can count on boomers to be very involved in their grandchildren's education. We want to help our grandchildren do well in school, giving them even better educational opportunities than we had while growing up. "It's not just about how can you make your grandchildren more effective in what they're trying to do," says J. Walker Smith, a managing partner at market research firm Yankelovich Partners and coauthor of Rocking the Ages. "[It's] about how you can help your grandchildren be better people."

> **Debra Schmitt:** *"I've been able to build up a bank account for my three grandchildren [the oldest is seven]. Now I can give them things I couldn't even give my own children. For instance, I'm able to pay for them to go to private school, which I consider the most important thing that I could do for them."*

Never before has the need been greater for grandparents to help pay for their grandchildren's education. In 2003, according to the College Board, the cost of tuition and fees at a public college or university soared 14 percent, the largest increase in thirty years. That same year, the average cost of one year at a state school, including room and board, was $10,636 and a whopping $26,854 at a private school. Imagine what it will cost years from now when your grandchild heads off to college. Now is the time to start building a war chest for college savings. Even though your financial worth is a few zeros shy of Bill Gates's, you still should start an education fund for your grand-child. Here are a few of the more popular ways for grandparents:

State 529 Investment Plans

It's a low-cost tax-advantaged way for anyone, such as grandparents, to save for a child's college education. When you invest in the plan (it has a limit of about $230,000 in many states), earnings on your invest-ment are tax-free as long as the money is used for college expenses. Every state sponsors at least one plan.

"It's basically a way to put money away—sort of like an expanded educational IRA," says Wallem. "It's much more powerful and flexible than the prepaid college tuition plans. You can use it for any public or private school anywhere, as long as the school meets the qualifications for post-high school educational purposes. It's fairly liberal as to what is considered college expenses. If you live in New Jersey and your child wants to go to school in Colorado, it still works."

A grandparent can contribute as much as $11,000 a year ($22,000 for couples) without triggering the federal gift tax. If you hit the lot-tery, you can also jump-start your grandchild's 529 plan by contribut-ing as much as $55,000—or $110,000 for a married couple—at one time, spreading the gift tax exclusion over the next five years.

Eligible expenses include tuition for a part-time, full-time, or distance-learning program, fees, books and supplies, and room and board.

"Each state has teamed up with an investment company," Wallem explains. "In some cases, there are state tax advantages to using the plan from your state, but you also have to take into consideration, 'Do I like the investment options that this state plan offers?' You can join the plan from any state you want.

"The beauty of the 529 plan is its flexibility. If your grandchild grows up and doesn't want to go to college, you can change the benefi-ciary to another qualifying family member—another grandchild, your spouse, or even you—without triggering taxes or penalties." However, if you take money out for noncollege expenses, you'll have to pay income taxes on your earnings, plus a 10 percent penalty.

Most 529 plans offer age-based portfolios that invest heavily in stocks when the beneficiary is young and then gradually move to more conservative investments as the child approaches college age. You need to decide if you want to invest in a 529 plan on your own or through a financial planner. "Many people would rather have an investment expert tell them how to invest the money because the plans can get complicated," says Wallem. "An adviser can help you find the plan that's right for you."

For more information, go to www.savingforcollege.com or www.collegesavings.org.

State-Sponsored Prepaid College Tuition Plans

A state-sponsored prepaid college tuition plan offers the promise of a reasonably-priced education for your grandchild. An investment in a prepaid tuition plan allows you to buy all or part of your grandchild's future tuition at roughly today's prices.

It works like this: You lock in tuition rates at a state college or university by paying a lump sum or making monthly payments. The state pools the money and invests it, then agrees to pay the tuition when your grandchild starts college.

The plan protects against tuition inflation. From 1998 to 2003, the average tuition at a public college rose more than 40 percent. As is the case with 529 savings plans, gains on investments aren't taxed as long as the money is used for college. Some states let you deduct part of your contribution from state taxes.

You have to be a resident to participate in a state plan, and not all states offer prepaid plans. Also, some of these plans are not backed by the full faith and credit of the states that sponsor them. If the plan runs into financial problems, it may not be able to pay the full cost of future tuition. If your grandchild chooses to go to a private or out-of-state school, you can use the money in your prepaid account to pay costs. But because the amount will be limited to the cost of tuition in your state, you might come up short. If your grandchild chooses to go to some unaccredited school like The Mahareshi School of Levitation, you can get your money back. Many public or private schools are establishing their own tax-exempt tuition programs.

Be aware that as of early 2004, five states had suspended or closed down their prepaid tuition plans (although they promise to take care of those who were already in the plans). Other states have warned that if tuition rates continue to soar, they might also be forced to close.

Independent 529 Plan

This is a prepaid tuition plan sponsored by a large nationwide group of more than 200 private colleges. Every member college offers a certificate discount so that you effectively pay less than today's prices for your grandchild's tuition. The amount of tuition you've prepurchased won't change no matter what happens to the stock market—or how much college tuitions rise. You don't have to decide on the college when you purchase the plan. Your prepaid tuition will be valid at any participating college once your grandchild enrolls. The Independent 529 Plan offers the same federal tax benefits as any 529 prepaid tuition plan or state-sponsored 529 plan.

It makes economic sense for you to buy when your grandchild is young because all member colleges offer a discount to certificate purchasers of at least one-half of one percent per year off the current tuition. The value of the certificate discount compounds between the time you purchase a certificate and when you redeem it. That means the longer you hold a certificate, the greater the value of your purchase.

If you elect to participate in an automatic purchase plan, you can buy a certificate for as little as $25 per month. Certificate owners must contribute at least $500 in total purchases within the first two years of the initial purchase date. The upper limit of contribution is $137,500 per beneficiary.

For more information, go to www.independent529plan.org.

Coverdell Education Savings Account

A Coverdell, formerly known as the Education IRA, might be best for you if you have limited funds. With a Coverdell, depending on your adjusted gross income, you can contribute up to $2,000 for each grand-child. Like a 529 plan, earnings are usually not subject to federal income tax. Unlike a 529, however, a Coverdell is not deductible from your state income tax.

One advantage is that you control how the money is invested. State 529 plans are usually managed by financial firms that offer limited investment options. A Coverdell allows you to invest in a favorite stock or low-expense index fund. However, you can't get your money back once the account is opened, as you can with a 529.

Be aware that if the parents are also contributing to a Coverdell, and your combined contributions total more than $2,000 in any one year, your grandchild must pay a 6 percent excise tax on excess contributions. Make sure you consult the parents before setting up a Coverdell.

Uniform Gift to Minors (UGMA) and Uniform Transfers to Minors (UTMA)

If you want to help build a nest egg for your grandchild to use as he sees fit when he's old enough, one of the easiest ways is to set up a Uniform Gift to Minors (UGMA) or Uniform Transfers to Minors (UTMA) custodial account, says Wallem. This lets you create an investment account for your grandchild without the hassles and expense of setting up a trust through an attorney.

"Even if you have a modest net worth and aren't in a position to give very much, yet you want to give something, the UGMA approach might be right for you," says Wallem. "You probably don't want, or need, to go through the legal expense of creating a trust."

To establish a custodial account, you must appoint a custodian (you or another trustee) and provide the name and social security number of your grandchild. The custodian has the fiduciary responsibility to manage the money in a prudent fashion for the benefit of the minor.

Under an UGMA, you can give your grandchild an irrevocable gift of securities, cash, life insurance, and annuities. You choose what type of investments to make. For example, you can transfer or buy shares in a mutual fund for the custodial account. "That's very simple, very easy," Wallem says. "The only problem is that you have control over the account only until the child reaches the age of majority, which is eighteen in most states. Then he will have control of the money. That could be a hang-up. The grandparent says, 'I want the money to go for college' and the eighteen-year-old says, 'I want it to go toward a red Corvette.'

"If there's a good relationship between the teenager and grandparent, the teen likely will listen to the grandparent who says, 'I gave you this money for college and that's what I want you to use it for.' Hopefully the moral persuasion will work. But if the teen says, 'I am of age so give me the money,' you have to do it." (Can you imagine what you would have done with thousands of bucks when you turned eighteen?)

There are some possible tax consequences to the grandparent, however. The first $750 of unearned income from the child's investment is tax-free. The next $750 will be taxed at the child's rate if the child is under age fourteen. Any additional unearned income is taxed at the grandparent's rate until the child turns fourteen. At age fourteen and over, all income is taxed at the child's rate.

Under the Uniform Transfers to Minors Act (UTMA), you can transfer more than just bank deposits, securities, and insurance policies. An UTMA allows your grandchild to receive the transfer of any types of property such as real estate, partnership interests, patents, fine art, royalties, and intellectual property. Like an UGMA account, an UTMA gift is put in the name of a custodial adult on behalf of the minor. An UTMA, which in most cases considers the age of majority to be twenty-one, is slightly more flexible than an UGMA.

Always keep in mind that custodial accounts are considered assets of the grandchild, so when he's ready for college, it could impact his eligibility for financial aid and the amount that he could obtain.

Trusts

If you want total control of how your gifted money is spent, consider setting up a trust, which can be funded by existing money, life insurance policy proceeds, or other property. The beauty of a trust is that you dictate the terms. A basic trust will allow your grandchild to draw a certain amount of funds at certain times for certain reasons—all according to the terms you drew up in the trust. That way, when your grandchild reaches a certain age, he can't blow your money investing in plastic pink flamingos or a new line of Nehru jackets. The trust can be as simple or as complex as you want.

"There are different types of trusts with different features to them," says Wallem. "You should have one drafted by an attorney. A trust is usually driven by the tax situation of the person giving the money more so than of those who benefit from it."

You might find that your best bet is to just pay your grandchild's education bills at the time they are due. "Make sure to send the check directly to the school," says Wallem. "If you give the money to the parents, it becomes part of their assets, which likely would affect the way any financial aid is calculated for your grandchild."

No matter how you choose to help, set up a financial plan now; don't wait until you're as crotchety as Grandpa Amos McCoy. "If you're planning on putting the money in an investment, do it now and not later so it will have more time to grow and compound," says Wallem. "Having an additional ten to fifteen years for that money to grow can make a huge difference as opposed to giving the same amount of money just when your grandchild gets ready for college.

"If the child has quite a few years before using that money, an aggressive growth mutual fund makes a lot of sense. If you want to add to your grandchild's mutual fund, do it on a frequent basis, like monthly, rather than all at once at the end of the year. You could have a slightly better return on your investment that way."

Make sure that you read all the information about a prospective investment and fully understand what you're buying, adds Wallem.

Even a modest investment strategy can pay off for your grandchild. Let's say you put $100 a month away for him for eighteen years—a total of $21,600. At an average return of 8 percent per year, the fund will have grown to $48,006 (not factoring any deductions for taxes or transaction expenses). At 3 percent inflation, that sum would be the equivalent of $27,994 in today's dollars.

Tom (Grandpa) Andersen: *"I put two dollars a day away for my granddaughter Sara. I increase that total by twenty-five cents* *a year. It's all invested so that when she graduates high school, she'll have enough for college."*

Wallem suggests you consider a technique called dollar cost averaging, which involves a psychological factor in investing. "If you put money in on a regular basis, it's easier to accept those times when the market goes down because you are buying shares cheaper. If you put in $2,000 once a year and then the market goes down, you feel awful. But if you invest $167 a month there won't be such an adverse psychological impact.

"There's also a learning dimension to this for your grandchild. Our educational system does a poor job of preparing young people to manage their own money when they are adults. You can help change that now. Depending on your situation, you might consider buying a good, broadly-diversified mutual fund investing in companies you think your grandchild will be interested in.

"Maybe by the time he's ten years old, he will be interested enough to check the paper and learn the basics of investing. It's an abstract concept for a young person. But if you can turn him into a saver and an investor at a young age, he might save or invest wisely when he starts earning his own money. He's less likely to spend it all. You will have done that child a huge favor."

You definitely should consider your own tax situation before gifting to anyone, he adds. "Let's say you owned some shares of Microsoft that you bought at five dollars and it's now worth fifty dollars. You can gift those shares of stock to your grandchild without having to pay taxes on the gain in the shares. However, your grandchild will have to pay any capital gains taxes whenever the stock is sold."

Even if you're not ready for trusts, UGMAs, and UTMAs, you may have assets and valuable personal items that you want to give directly to your grandchildren at some future time. If so, include those items in your will. (You do have one, don't you?) Putting your wishes down in writing helps ensure that your mint condition Pez dispenser collection or your cherished Ginny Doll collection will go directly to your grandkids.

With banks, brokerage houses, insurance companies, and mutual fund companies all competing for your business with a variety of financial products, gifts, and services, where do you go? Before you do anything, says Wallem, consult with a professional, such as a Certified Financial Planner. "The good CFP will act as the old family doctor. Like the general practitioner, the CFP determines your situation, walks you through the alternatives, and then, if need be, refers you to a good specialist. For example, if it's determined that you have a complex situation, the CFP might put you in contact with a trust attorney or an estate planning attorney. The CFP looks at the broad picture and coordinates the specialists that will best serve you in your situation. Personal chemistry between you and the CFP is important because you need to feel comfortable with someone who is suggesting to you where to invest your money."

Another reason to talk with an expert is because the tax code changes about as often as Madonna alters her looks. Plus, you need to know the tax ramifications of any financial gift you give.

"It's such an individual situation," says Wallem. "There are boomer grandparents who have done well financially and are looking at estate taxes and asking how they can pass their assets on to the next generation. But we run into boomers who have lost their jobs or are in a career change. Many of them are worried about having enough to retire on. That's really their main focus."

If you're torn between saving for your grandchildren's education and your own retirement, most financial advisers urge you to make your retirement fund the top priority. According to a 2003 AARP survey, 68 percent of workers between the ages of fifty and seventy plan to work in retirement or never retire—many because they haven't saved enough.

"You need to take care of your own needs first," says Wallem. "If you're not in a position to help your grandchildren with their education, they can tap into other sources such as grants, scholarships, work-study programs, and loans. On the other hand, whatever help you can offer will definitely be worthwhile."

The bottom line: Financially help your grandchildren as early as you can. No matter what you contribute, let it come from the heart.

A Groovy Kind of Love

Becoming the Best Grandparent

Face Time

IF YOU WANT TO BE A SUPER twenty-first-century grandparent, you must give your grandchildren two treasured gifts. No, not a six-foot-tall teddy bear from Neiman Marcus or a kid-sized, gas-powered Lamborghini from FAO Schwarz. The gifts we're talking about are the same ones that good grandparents have been sharing with their kids' kids since the beginning of civilization. And they cost nothing.

"The two best things you can give to your grandchildren are love and time," declares Dr. T. Berry Brazelton. "The danger is in trying to seduce your grandchildren by giving them bigger or more expensive gifts, hoping they'll remember you better. They aren't going to remember you for things like that anyway. The great reward of being a grandparent is that your grandchildren, like your mother and father, love you for yourself, and for no other reason."

Giving grandkids your love is easy. Giving them your time . . . well, that can be tough, especially since you need to spend time with each one of them alone.

If your grandchildren are typical, they're experiencing much less face time with their parents than you did with yours when you were a kid. Out of necessity, most of today's parents are leading Mad Hatter, beat-the-clock lives, and must opt for "quality time" squeezed in somewhere between the tuna casserole, the dirty laundry, the sales report revisions, the boss' phone calls, and the kids' bath and bedtime.

Your grandchildren need your undivided attention, and with it your warm touch, knowing eyes, and sympathetic ears. In return, you'll get from them something much more meaningful and precious than just a sound bite.

In his Grandparent Study, Dr. Arthur Kornhaber found that grandchildren rarely mention things their grandparents had given them except for heirlooms. Instead, they talk about what their grandparents did *with* them.

"You really don't get to know the grandchildren unless you spend some time alone with them," says Dr. Susan Ginsberg, editor and publisher of the national newsletter *Work & Family Life*. "That's a very important point. Kids usually don't interact with grandparents as much when the parents are around. You need to make an effort—however often it happens—to spend time alone with each kid so you both can get to know each other better."

That means, she says, spending time alone with one grandchild at a time. One-on-one. Just you and your grandchild. Not your spouse, not the other grandkids. Only the two of you.

It's the best way to build a deep, loving relationship and to make meaningful, lasting memories. If you need inspiration in pulling this off, press the rewind button in your head and replay those moments with your grandparents or significant elders who were important to you as a child. What was special about them in your life? What images and feelings are you experiencing in this rerun? How can you emulate or adapt those scenes to fit your role as a grandparent?

> **Kathryn:** "*Some of the moments I remember most about my Grandpa Clyde are the simplest ones. One time when I was five and visiting on the farm, he took me to town in his truck to the combine repair shop. He gave me a nickel for the Coke machine (the kind where the green bottle slid down the chute after you turned the handle). While I sat quietly drinking my Coke (which Mom never let me have), the welder fixed Grampa's broken combine part. This moment may not seem like much but it has stayed with me for all these years. I think it's because it was the first time the two of us spent time together alone.*
>
> "*We did lots of things together after that. We walked in the fields where he showed me how corn reproduces and pointed out the difference between a female and male melon blossom. He taught me how to bait a hook with a big juicy earthworm and use it to catch fish in his lake. When I was thirteen, he let me drive*

his truck around the barnyard. He didn't mind that the transmission cried out in protest during my futile attempts to shift gears.

"*What mattered was that I spent time with him alone, not with my sister or my two brothers. I spent a lot of time alone with Grandma Melba too. My grandparents thought I—as well as each of their other twenty-five grandchildren—was special. Those were the happiest days of my childhood.*"

Grandmother Karen O'Connor, author of *Innovative Grandparenting*, wrote:

> People of all ages are hungry for undivided personal time with one of their loved ones. Grandkids want to feel special and grandparents want to connect in a personal way.
>
> But somehow life—the daily routine—gets in the way. It doesn't require money or even much time. It does require, however, that you be there, present to the child as a person who cares, who listens, who empathizes, who affirms, who is fun, and who is easy to be with.
>
> That can take place over a pancake breakfast at a local diner or on the floor of your bedroom playing dolls. It can happen while you drive to the grocery store or hardware store or in a shared moment during a symphony or play. Whatever you choose, make sure it's something for just the two of you. Sitting on the park bench reading a newspaper while your grandchild plays alone in the sand at the park is not what I'm talking about. Dropping your grandchild off at a library event for children and then picking him up later doesn't count either.
>
> No matter how busy you are, if you want to have a close relationship with your grandchildren, it's essential that you find ways to interact with them one at a time.

Here are five crucial roles that you should play when you're alone with your grandchild:

The Playmate

"We need to get away from buying the newest Barbie Doll every time we visit the grandchildren and getting only one hour's play out of it," says

Jody Martin, curriculum specialist for the Children's World Learning Center. "We need to get down on their level and just play with them."

Play whatever game or make-believe diversion your grandchild enjoys, says sociologist Susan Newman, a grandmother of five. Go into the child's world and do something that's of interest to her. If she wants to finger-paint, then finger-paint with her. If she wants to toboggan down Suicide Hill, do it. "It will be so meaningful," says Newman. "When my son was about four, his grandmother came to visit. He wanted to play with his toy newspaper truck so she got down on the floor with him and she made little newspaper bundles and they loaded them in the truck and took them out. My son is grown now, and he still talks about that time with her."

It's never too early to start playing. If your grandchild is a baby, simply rock her, read or sing to her, take her out in a stroller. With a toddler or preschooler, sit on the floor and roll a ball back and forth; play tag, hide-and-seek, or horsey; make sand castles, play with her toys and dolls. With a slightly older child, try baking cookies together, swim, hike, blow bubbles, wrestle, jump rope, play board games, fish, hike, do puzzles, tell jokes. The key is to have unadulterated fun. There doesn't have to be a reason to do it other than it seems like a great idea. Don't even have a hidden agenda of trying to teach her something. Follow the Beach Boys' philosophy: Fun, fun, fun!

> **Carrie (Maw Maw) Dulcette:** *"Every time I see my grandson, I have to get down on my hands and knees and play grizzly bear with him."*

> **Gran Nan:** *"Bree loves to sing and I do too. So we're always singing the most nonsensical songs—most of them made up on the spot."*

> **Judy (Grammy) Ernest, in the *Cleveland Plain Dealer*:** *"For my birthday they [her grandchildren's parents] gave me a sled. As I zipped down the hill on a snowy February day next to my grandson, I felt like a five-year-old. There's nothing like playing with a grandchild to make you feel like a kid."*

One of the joys of playing with our grandsons Chad and Danny is watching the world through their eyes. When they were toddlers, we saw their sheer happiness over popping a floating soap bubble, picking up a lost shiny penny, or stomping in a puddle. We heard their squeals of discovery over seeing an ant carry a crumb, feeling the vibrations of a purring cat, or listening to the tones from touching a phone's keypad.

"Parents are so concerned with molding the child's mind and helping her grow up that they don't take the time to see things through her eyes," says Dr. Perry Buffington. "Grandparents don't want to rush grandkids into growing up too fast because they enjoy playtime with the kids."

Find out what your grandchildren like to do—then do it with them.

> **Allan:** *"Now that our grandsons are grade-schoolers, they see a world where everything is a fun contest—firing squirt guns or snowballs, playing hoops or soccer, racing on Rollerblades or ice skates. The trouble is they're getting so darn good, they're beating me even when I'm not taking it easy on them."*

The Friend

Appreciate all your grandchild's strengths and flaws. She needs someone who's there to give her unqualified support and understanding. Offer encouragement and compassion. Lend an ear, listen to her fears and anxieties, and offer advice when asked. Let her feel so comfortable with you that she could tell you anything. She can count on you to be there in good times and bad. If her self-esteem is shaky because of constant criticism from parents or teachers, you need to build up her ego. You can best take on this role of a friend if you let her get close to you.

"Fun is a fine thing in a grandparent, but the key is approachability," says Dr. Buffington. "You need to be there for her. Grandparents typically are far better listeners than parents. Your ability to be a friend doesn't have any strings attached."

> **Linda (Mimi) Gray:** *"I'm amazed not only at what comes out of her [granddaughter's] mouth, but what comes out of mine when we're together. We talk about everything. She's only five and already she knows my life story."*

When you talk to your grandchild, you need to be involved enough in her life so that you know what questions to ask, says Newman. "That's when you need the parents to help you. Talk to them first so you know what's happening in your grandchild's life—what's going on in her playgroup or in preschool. Then you can have a fulfilling conversation that relates to her. You'll be able to ask the right questions."

To get more out of the relationship, ask your grandchild open-ended questions, suggests Martin. "If you ask questions that can be answered in one word, that's what you'll likely get. If you ask, 'How are you?' or 'How was the movie?' you'll probably hear 'Fine.' It's better to ask questions like, 'What was your favorite part of the movie?' and follow up with 'Why?' It leads to so many other questions and a nice conversation. Another way to get her talking is to say something like, 'Tell me about the animals you saw at the zoo.'"

Also, it's important to talk about yourself because that fosters a two-way relationship, Martin adds.

The Teacher

"Many grandparents feel they have to stock their houses with games and toys for their grandchildren, when children actually learn so many other things just by being with their grandparents," says Dr. Kornhaber.

Do you have a skill or a hobby? Are you into cooking, car repair, computers, drumming circles, painting, music, sailing, horseback riding, candle-making, surfing? Whatever pastime you enjoy, introduce it to your grandchild. Perhaps your passion will rub off on her. So often, the younger generation learns from the older generation.

"As mentors, grandparents can spark a grandchild's imagination, providing motivation and inspiration by just being there," says Dr. Kornhaber. "These lessons often have a lifelong influence." The Grandparent Study reported that knowledge, skills, and attitudes acquired from grandparents stuck more permanently than things grandchildren picked up from other sources.

Ray (Papa) Villwock: *"I passed down to my sons my love for fishing but not to the extent that I had hoped. However, as a* grandfather, I can spend more time fishing with my grandkids and pass down to them my passion for the sport."

Keri (Grams) Lytle: "My hobby is pottery and Maddie, who's four, likes to play with clay and mold it into intriguing shapes. She has some great talent. I'm helping her learn how to throw pots."

Sandi (Grammy) Kingman: "I love to bake. My grandmother taught me and now I'm teaching my grandchildren. I'm teaching each one to make his or her own specialty—strawberry-rhubarb pie for Staci and pecan pie for Robby."

Dan (Grandpa) Skinner: "My wife and I have a couple of '69 Camaros and are members of the Bad to the Bone Cruisers Car Club. For [their two-year-old granddaughter] Victoria's Easter basket, we got her a tackle box filled with Hot Wheels. Victoria loved it."

For most young children the chance to observe the world is a great learning experience. You can show your grandchild the wonders of the most common, ordinary, and everyday things in life.

"Go on an outing together," suggests Martin. "Spend time in nature just listening and observing. Smell flowers, look for bugs, notice the weather. Your grandchild will ask lots of questions for you to answer."

Picnics are a wonderful time to share nature with your grandchild. Watching ducks paddle in a pond, clouds float overhead, or squirrels gather nuts help teach her a respect for the world around her.

Elly (Granny) Shodell: "[Her grandson] Andy's life is extremely regimented and he has all these activities, so there's little down time for him to be just a kid. When we see him, we let him climb trees and play in the dirt and do things that he's not otherwise allowed to do or has the opportunity to do in his gated community. His parents hate ants and insects and squishy stuff, so when we visit, we purposely try to find every insect we can and let Andy get used to them. We dissect the dead ones and get him out of the mindset that everything has to be sterile and hygienic."

Nana Lana: *"I like to take the grandkids out at night and snuggle on a blanket in a nearby field and gaze at the stars. I make up stories about the constellations and occasionally we make wishes when we see shooting stars."*

You can teach more than just skills or the world around us. You can teach by example, by setting the standards for the family in morals and values, by practicing your spiritual beliefs, and by honoring your family's culture and traditions.

"As a grandparent, you can teach lessons that go back several generations," says Dr. Buffington. "Because you are aware of your own mortality, you become more concerned with binding the generations. You become a better teacher of traditions and morality than the parents. The kids are watching you to some degree more than they are watching their parents.

"For some of us, that might mean cleaning up our act. Better late than never. It makes a difference."

The Comforter

When we were kids, we felt threatened by the atomic bomb. Remember "duck and cover" drills in school? Today, our grandchildren are growing up in a world threatened by terrorists who have no regard for human life. We grandparents can play a key role in making sure that our grandchildren feel safe and secure following a traumatic event such as the 9/11 terrorist attack.

"Talk with your grandchild in language she can understand," says Dr. Buffington. "Volunteer only enough information to answer her question, and don't confuse her with too many facts, figures, and details. Don't lie. Answer her questions in honest, straightforward language. Bambi's mom found it necessary to tell her fawn, 'Man has entered the forest.' Children can understand terms like 'mean' and 'evil.'" Talking about violent acts won't increase your grandchild's fear, but suppressing her feelings could.

Young children, especially preschoolers, easily can be upset or overwhelmed by what they see and hear on TV because they tend to confuse facts with their fantasies and fears, he says. "You need to help your grandchild keep things in perspective, especially when news footage is shown over and over. She might not realize that this is a single incident that's being rebroadcast.

"It's not unusual for a child to be clingy when a traumatic event hits. Allow her to express her feelings. Hug her and offer expressions of 'I love you' to reduce her fear, worry, and anxieties. Ask your grandchild, 'What can we do together to feel better?' She might want to draw pictures expressing her feelings or make something to give to a victim or family member.

"To get through these terrible times, your grandchild could use a spiritual anchor. You can be that powerful coping device. Express your faith, with your grandchild present, through your acts, words, deeds, and prayers."

If a traumatic event directly affects your grandchild—for example, the unexpected death of a friend or family member, a serious accident or illness, the breakup of her parents—you absolutely must be there to comfort and reassure her. Let her know that she can count on you, and that you will do whatever it takes to ease the pain she's feeling.

The Family Historian

When you show grandchildren their family roots, they learn they are part of a larger, living entity. You provide them with a new perspective in understanding how things of today link up with the past. Above all, you help them learn about the family history, their ancestors, and the origin of the family name.

Kay Harvey: *"My grandmother used to tell me stories, and now I realize her voice is my voice and the two of us have become one."*

"Grandparents are the family archivists, providing grandchildren with a link to the past through stories of relatives long dead as well as passing on family ways, rites, and rituals," says Dr. Kornhaber.

This role takes some effort. Collect photos of your parents and grandparents and put them in an album or on a CD or DVD. That way you can point out to your grandchildren from whom they got their wiry hair, their musical voice, their fiery temper.

If you haven't already, collect family heirlooms and things from your own past. Make videos of any living elderly relatives, tape oral histories, gather any family journals and letters. Let the kids rummage through the attic, basement, or storage shed. (You might want to get rid of the hookah and lava lamp. What are you keeping those for anyway?) Children find the most wonderful treasures in these places. You can spend countless hours pulling out memorabilia and telling fascinating stories attached to each special item.

"Kids love it when they look at photo albums and hear stories about their parents when they were kids," says Martin.

It's healthy to show off the pictures of you with bell-bottoms and the tie-dyed clothes, Dr. Buffington adds. "It's no different than George Washington's white wig. It was a statement of the times. Tell them about the Vietnam War. Tell them how your generation started Earth Day and advocated more freedom of mind and choice, and fueled the women's movement."

You serve as a human video of the family's personal saga of experiences and events (some of which, no doubt, you'll want to edit out). You get to explain how your life was affected by Haight-Ashbury, the Chicago Eight trial, the Arab Oil Embargo, whatever.

Tom (Grandpa) Andersen: *"I have a collection of front pages of important events that happened during my life—JFK's assassination, Neil Armstrong walking on the moon, Nixon resigning. I will use them as starting points for me to talk about my life to my grandkids when they're old enough to understand."*

Kathryn: *"I'm marking all the heirlooms that I have from my parents, grandparents, and great-grandparents. I'm sticking labels underneath the items so that my grandkids will know where these things came from—and before I forget."*

Kirk Leiter: *"Every family photo is on computer disc so hopefully it will always be there for all my grandchildren to enjoy. I've made several copies."*

Making Time

You say you don't have time to be a playmate, friend, comforter, teacher, and historian to each grandchild? Find the time. No, *make* the time. What can be more important than playing a major role in the life of a child? Don't be one of those boomers who's trying to jam more "me time" into an already crammed schedule because you're freaked out that life is passing you by too quickly. If you don't get involved with your grandchildren right now, what will pass you by is your opportunity to make a positive impact in their lives.

> **Sara Schotland, an attorney in Washington, D.C., in**
> ***American Demographic:*** *"I would never leave the office except*
> *in an emergency [when she was raising her children]. But today,*
> *even though I'm still an active partner in my firm, the priority, time,*
> *and attention for my granddaughter is without limit. I've left the*
> *office at 3 P.M. at least ten times this year to tend to her needs."*

If you have the time for one more set on the clay courts or one more vodka and tonic at happy hour, you can make the time for your grandchild. Sometimes it takes a little planning or flexibility to create opportunities to be with a little one.

"Being with your grandchild doesn't require as much time as you think," says Newman. "Children envision time differently than adults do. A half hour or hour may seem short to us, but to a child who is enjoying what she's doing, that time is expanded for her."

You can always make time. For example, if you're at a family gathering, sneak away after the meal with one of the grandkids and go for a walk—alone. Or take her to a nearby park for a few minutes so she can play on the swings. "You might be amazed at how special a moment you'll both have even in a short span of time," says Newman.

"If you have simple chores to do, do them together. Perhaps you could get a child-size rake for her and let her help you rake the yard. Take her to the grocery store with you because it can be a wonderful learning experience. You can point out shapes, colors, and sizes, and, depending on her age, even some basic math. Take her with you to the bank, post office, gas station, construction site, or wherever you need to go for your errands. Just being together is the important thing."

Dr. Ginsberg sometimes takes her granddaughter to the office or to exercise class so she can see what her nana does for work and for fun. "It allows me to spend more time with her. Anything you can do to involve your grandchildren in your life, do it."

If possible, find ways you can alter your work schedule so you can be with your grandchild for a special event such as a birthday party or a recital. Maybe you can finish the management report at home, swap shifts with a fellow employee, or get someone to cover for you at the store.

> **Debra Schmitt, on *Good Morning America*:** *"When the grandkids visit our lakeside home, my husband and I take them for a run first thing in the morning. After that, they eat breakfast, go swimming in the lake, swing on the swing sets, and then take a nap. Later, we watch movies and have popcorn. If I was an older grandma, I don't think I'd have the energy to be so involved in their lives. My daughter loves it—she's happy to have parents who can do so much with her kids."*

To get the most out of your time together, become a grandparent who specializes in something fun, Newman suggests. "Tie it in with something you need to accomplish or that you really like to do. For example, if you enjoy gardening, then become the gardening grandparent.

"Be a specialist so that your grandchildren think of you in a special way. Don't make yourself the gift-buying grandparent; make something of yourself. My five grandchildren think of me as the activity grandmother. We're always doing something—hunting for four-leaf clovers, taking a ride on a train, building a snowman, carving pumpkins. Those short blocks of time like that can leave lasting impressions.

"The best way to make the most of your limited time is to plan ahead. Figure out what you're going to do before you get together with your grandchild. It doesn't have to be anything complex. The more interaction, the more lasting the impression. Those moments are going to stand out in her mind.

"It doesn't matter what the activity is, just be totally involved and focused with your grandchild, which some parents have such difficulty doing because they are spread so thin. If you have only a half hour, do what she wants to do.

"If you come into her house, sit down, and turn on the TV while she's in the room, that's not quality time. It's only good time if you are paying attention to her and there's interaction.

"When you're together, by the way, take lots of photographs to build a memory bank in her mind. Toddlers aren't necessarily going to remember all the fun they had with you."

If possible, set up a video camera and record the whole afternoon. Children love to watch themselves over and over again. The tape also will capture that special day forever.

Diane Marquette: *"When I am with my stepgrandsons, I want the clock to stand still. The time I spend with them is so precious to me that I want to savor every moment and I want them to remember with happiness what we have done during our time together. I want them to recall the fun we had and the things that they learned."*

Reading to Your Grandchild

Of all the activities that a grandparent can do, one of the most important and rewarding is reading to your grandchild. Everyone benefits. You both spend precious time together, and you help her develop a love of books and the written word. Reading builds a foundation for future success in school and acts to prevent her from overdosing on TV and videos. Children who have been read to become better readers.

Martin and the Children's World Learning Center offer these tips to help you foster a positive reading experience for your grandchild:

- Remember that just spending time reading to her is more important than what is read.
- Eliminate distractions (TV, radio, phone, etc.) when you read to her.

- Find a comfortable place to read—a couch, easy chair, bed, or beanbag chair.

- Help her select the book she wants to read.

- Provide her with varied books of interest to her. Says Martin, "Books that make sounds and have rhythm or show pictures of babies and animals appeal to infants. Toddlers enjoy books with textured pictures and with objects they can name. Sesame Street and Barney stories are popular with preschoolers as are books about other children. Five- and six-year-olds are intrigued with magical stories, fairy tales, and books about dinosaurs and animals."

- Don't just open the book and start reading. "There's so much more to learn from a book than just reading it. Spend time talking about it first. Discuss the cover, show her the name of the author and explain that the person wrote it. Flip through the book and look at the pictures and have her point out the colors and objects. Ask her such things as, 'Can you find all the squares in the picture?' 'How many times does the word 'the' appear on this page?'"

- Let her participate in the reading by turning pages, saying words, lifting flaps, and asking questions.

- Discuss the book after you've read it. "Ask her, 'How would you end the story?' 'What character would you like to be?' Suggest that she draw a picture about the story."

- Use the book to spur conversation with her about such topics as day care, friends, likes and dislikes, fun experiences, pets, etc.

- Keep books handy and stored in such a way that your grandchild can easily find the book she wants to read.

Creating Traditions and Rituals

As a grandparent, you should maintain or create family traditions and rituals, say the experts. In a changing world of uncertainty, traditions and rituals provide the family—especially children—with something regular, consistent, reliable, cherished, and predictable to look forward to.

Carrie (Maw Maw) Dulcette: *"On New Year's Day, the whole family jumps into our pond—no matter how cold the temperature is. Even the little ones, after the age of four, go in. This will be Sean's first time. He'll finally realize what a crazy family he's born into."*

"Rituals and traditions help form a family's identity," says family expert Dr. Gregory Sanders. "They provide important opportunities for families to express their strengths and build their relationships. I have my students write about their family traditions and rituals. Many students say these are very powerful and positive mechanisms for keeping their family going. They particularly refer to Thanksgiving and Christmas as the times their family most often experiences their rituals and traditions.

"Once a ritual is established, it causes some family disagreements if anyone tries to alter it in any way. However, we're not as good at practicing them as we have been in the past and we're losing out because of that."

Dr. Buffington agrees. "Traditions are more important than ever before," he says. "People crave traditions and cherish these moments. Kids remember moments. If a child knows that every December we are going out to cut down a Christmas tree because it's a family tradition, then that consistency provides comfort to him.

"If your family adopted a tradition, chances are your adult child is teaching it to your grandkid. It's a linkage you have. A good grandparent will take the traditions that have already been implemented and try to make them better. If your family does not have any traditions or rituals, then for God's sake, create some. Your job as a grandparent is to create moments. It's essential. You must have something as a link to the past. One of the reasons people want these links is that the present is so tenuous."

It's also important to foster or create a ritual that's between you and your grandchild—a special activity that just the two of you do together on certain occasions.

Allan: *"Whenever the grandkids come to visit us in the North Carolina mountains, we 'collect' a waterfall. During each trip, we hike to a different waterfall and have our photo taken there."*

Ray (Papa) Villwock: *"I took [his grandson] Max to the Florida Marlins Opening Day game when he was five months old, and he's been to every Opening Day game since. He's still too young to fully appreciate it. But when he's grown up, he'll be able to say that since he was born, he's been to every Marlins' Opening Day with his grandfather."*

Spoiling Your Grandchild

A classic bumper sticker reads: "Grandparents and grandchildren get along so well because they both have the same enemies." We nanas and papas get to conspire with our grandkids to do all the little things that Mom and Dad normally would frown upon.

Whoopi Goldberg, to the Associated Press: *"I spoil those kids [her two grandchildren] rotten. I give them anything they want and let them do anything they want. I teach them naughty songs and then send them off home to be disciplined."*

We shouldn't have to worry about our grandkids staying up past bedtime, gobbling too many sweets, or wearing mismatched clothes. We're supposed to concentrate on the fun stuff. This is our big reward for all those carpools, scout meetings, orthodontic appointments, PTA bake sales, Little League games, and piano lessons that dominated our conversation (and, for many of us, our lives) when we were raising our kids. This is the payback for all the times we had to say no, to send our kids to their rooms, to make them do their chores. Now we get to say yes to our grandkids, to indulge their every whim, and basically to have a blast.

Glenn (Pee Paw) Reed: *"A moment with my grandsons brightens a week at a time and explains all those moments when my parents fawned over my kids."*

"Some parents envy the relationship their children have with the grandparents," says Dr. Kornhaber. "Behavior that might be regarded as spoiling a child may, from another viewpoint, be recognized as simply an extension of the affection that many grandparents lavish on their grandchildren."

> **Michelle (Grammy) Davies:** *"I can sum up my role as a grandmother in a few words: 'To spoil my grandkids rotten!'"*

You'll probably get some flak from the parents for spoiling their child, but, hey, what can they do? Ground you? When we baby-sat Chad for five days while his parents took a much-needed vacation before Danny was born, we indulged him, no doubt about it. Okay, so maybe we went a little overboard, because on the first day after the parents returned home, his mother needed to send him to "time-out" three times. But Allison and Dan didn't complain about our spoiling him. They knew that was a small price to pay for their getaway. In fact, they sent us a gift certificate to an upscale restaurant as a thank-you. Although we were pleased with the thoughtful gesture, didn't they know that we would've paid them to baby-sit for Chad?

How Do You Want to Be Remembered?

So, what kind of nana or papa will you be? You can probably best answer that question by asking yourself another question: How do I want my grandchildren to remember me? Once you answer that, all you have to do is turn that thought into reality.

> **Ray (Papa) Villwock:** *"How do I want to be remembered? As the papa who was a lot of fun to be with and loved life."*

> **Jane (Nana) Trebble:** *"I want to be the grandma who gave her grandkids warm memories and a happy childhood."*

> **Dr. Anya (Baba) Luchow Liberman:** *"I want them to think of me as involved and loving; someone who was always there for them and listened to them. A fun grandma. An Auntie Mame grandma."*

> **David (Pop-Pop) Pilgrim:** *"The hip-hop Pop-Pop."*

Nana on the Net: *"I intend to be the grandparent who can provide my grandchildren with stability in times of crisis."*

Sue (Nana) Crawford: *"I want to be remembered as the fun grandma."*

Jane (Grandmom) Whitfield: *"To be someone who is genuine, sincere, and supportive of my grandchildren."*

Michelle (Grammy) Davies: *"The grammy who can make anything the grandkids want—from cookies to toys—magically appear."*

Jane (Nona) Haglund: *"I want to be [her grandson] Anson's pal and confidante. I just want to be anything and everything to him."*

Carrie (Maw Maw) Dulcette: *"I'm fixing to be the craziest, silliest, funnest grandma this family has ever had."*

Kathryn: *"I want to be a great big warm human security blanket for my grandkids."*

Allan: *"For my grandkids, I hope to be a mix of Soupy Sales, Mr. Wizard, Buffalo Bob, Pinky Lee, Captain Kangaroo, and Bozo the Clown."*

Who Can I Turn To?

Resources for Nanas and Papas

Grandparent Organizations

FOR CLEARINGHOUSES OF VALUABLE INFORMATION, advice, articles, links, and resources about grandparenting:

AARP Grandparent Information Center
601 E Street NW
Washington, DC 20049
888-687-2277 or 202-434-2296
www.aarp.org/confacts/programs/gic.html

The Foundation for Grandparenting
108 Farnham Road
Ojai, CA 93023
www.grandparenting.org

Grandparents Resource Center
Box 27064
Denver, CO 80227
303-980-5707
www.grc4usa.org

Generations United
1333 H Street NW
Suite 500 W
Washington, DC 20005
202-289-3979
www.gu.org

National Grandparents Day Council
1449 Antro Dr.
Loveland, CO 80538
970-669-7250
www.grandparents-day.com

Online Grandparenting Magazines and Sources

Grandloving
www.grandloving.com

Grandparents Magazine
www.grandparentsmagazine.net

Grand Boomers
www.grandboomers.com

Grandkids and Me
www.grandkidsandme.com

Grand Times
www.grandtimes.com

Grandparents.Com
www.grandparents.com

CyberGran
www.cyberparent.com/gran/

Grandparenting Today
www.uwex.edu/ces/flp/grandparent/index.html

FamilyEdge: Grandparents
www.familyedge.com/cgi-bin/kidsedge/scripts/familyedge/
grandparents/index.jsp

Other Resources

For a monthly newsletter providing information and practical advice on a wide range of family, job, and health issues that affect working parents and grandparents:

> *Work & Family Life*
> 317 Madison Avenue
> Suite 517
> New York, NY 10017
> 800-278-2579 (In New York, 212-557-3555)
> workfam@aol.com

For a guide with advice and a checklist of questions to discuss with your elderly parents (the great-grandparents) and a link to local resources that can help you deal with aging issues:

> Eldercare
> 800-677-1116
> www.eldercare.gov.

Grandparent Rights

For information concerning grandparent visitation rights and other legal issues affecting grandchildren:

> Grandparents Rights Organization
> 100 W. Long Lake Road
> Suite 250
> Bloomfield Hills, MI 48304
> 248-646-7177
> www.grandparentsrights.org

Grandparents United for Children's Rights
137 Larkin St.
Madison, WI 53705
608-238-8751
www.geocities.com/Heartland/Prairie/6866
sedun@inxpress.net

Grandparents Raising Grandchildren

Many grandparents often lack information about the range of support services and policies they need to fulfill their caregiving role. To help remedy this situation, a group of child and aging advocacy and research organizations, including AARP, the Children's Defense Fund, and the Child Welfare League of America, has prepared Kinship Care Fact Sheets for each state. They can provide you with a comprehensive list of kinship care family resources and services in your state along with information about key public benefit programs and kinship care laws. You can access this data by going to the Web sites of any of the above-mentioned organizations or by typing in "kinship care fact sheets" in your search engine.

For information, resources, support groups, and other material on child advocacy, child-rearing, and legal issues for grandparents who are raising grandchildren:

Child Welfare League of America
440 First Street, NW
3rd Floor
Washington, DC 20001
202-638-2952
www.cwla.org

The Children's Defense Fund
25 E Street NW
Washington, DC 20001
202-628-8787
www.childrensdefense.org

Casey Family Programs
1300 Dexter Avenue North
Floor 3
Seattle, WA 98109-3542
206-282-7300
www.casey.org

The Relatives as Parents Program
The Brookdale Foundation Group
950 Third Avenue
19th Floor
New York, NY 10022
www.brookdalefoundation.org

Grandparents as Parents (GAP)
Sylvie de Toledo
PO Box 964
Lakewood, CA 90714
818-789-1177 or 310-839-2548

Off Our Rockers
www.sonic.net/thom/oor

Grandparents and More
www.grandparentsandmore.com

GrandsPlace
www.grandsplace.com

Grandparenting Again
www.grandparentagain.com

Grandchild Safety

For information on toy safety, childproofing, and other child safety concerns:

U.S. Consumer Product Safety Commission (CPSC)
Washington, DC 20207-0001
301-504-6816
Hotline 800-638-2772
www.cpsc.gov

National Safe Kids Campaign
1301 Pennsylvania Avenue, NW
Suite 1000
Washington, DC 20004
202-662-0600
www.safekids.org

For recalls of consumer products, medicine, and food:

www.recalls.gov

Grandparent-Grandchild Travel

For grandparents looking for a fun, educational, and rewarding vacation with their grandchildren:

Elderhostel
11 Avenue de Lafayette
Boston, MA 02111
877-426-8056
www.elderhostel.org

Familyhostel
University of New Hampshire
6 Garrison Avenue
Durham, NH 03824
800-733-9753 (Outside United States, 603-862-1113)
www.learn.unh.edu/familyhostel

Sierra Club
85 Second Street
2nd Floor
San Francisco, CA 94105
415-977-5500
www.sierraclub.org

Grandtravel
1920 N Street, NW
Suite 200
Washington, DC 20036
800-247-7651 (In Washington, D.C., 202-785-8901)
www.grandtrvl.com

AFC Tours
11772 Sorrento Valley Road
Suite 101
San Diego, CA 92121
800-369-3693
www.afctours.com

Rascals in Paradise
One Daniel Burnham Court
Suite 105-C
San Francisco, CA 94109
415-921-7000
www.rascalsinparadise.com

For information about attending a week-long camp experience for
grandparents and grandchildren only, without the parents:

Grandparent-Grandchild Summer Camp
Sagamore Historic Adirondack Great Camp
PO Box 146
Raquette Lake, NY 13436
315-354-5311

Web site addresses often change. If you have trouble accessing any of these addresses, type in the name of the organization in your search engine for the latest address.

Selected Books on Grandparenting

The Grandparent Solution: Building a Family Team for Practical, Emotional, and Financial Success by Arthur Kornhaber, M.D. (John Wiley & Sons, 2004). Aimed at parents and how they can best utilize the strengths of the grandparents of their children for a happier home life.

Great Ideas for Grandkids! 150 Ways to Entertain, Educate, and Enjoy Your Grandchildren—Without Setting Foot in a Toy Store! by Peggy Epstein (McGraw-Hill/Contemporary, 2003) Provides more than 150 low-cost activities you can share with your grandkids using simple, readily available materials.

The Gift of Grandparenting by Thea Jarvis (Sorin Books, 2003). Encourages grandparents to receive laughter, disorder, and playtime from their grandchildren as spiritual gifts.

The Grandparent Guide by Arthur Kornhaber, M.D. (McGraw-Hill/Contemporary, 2002). Offers solid advice from the grandparenting guru on how nanas and papas can stay ahead of the curve of social change.

The Gift of Grandparenting: Building Meaningful Relationships with Your Grandchildren by Eric E. Wiggin and Gary D. Chapman (Tyndale House, 2001). Encourages grandparents to take an active role in creating strong spiritual and emotional family ties.

The Twelve Rules of Grandparenting: A New Look at Traditional Roles and How to Break Them by Susan M. Kettmann (Checkmark Books, 1999). Empowers grandparents to develop their own strategies for a positive impact on their grandchildren's lives.

To Grandma's House, We . . . Stay: When You Have to Stop Spoiling Your Grandchildren and Start Raising Them by Sally Houtman, M.S. (Studio 4 Productions, 1999). A guide for grandparents raising grandchildren that offers practical solutions to the real-life problems they face.

The Essential Grandparent: A Guide to Making a Difference by Dr. Lillian Carson (Health Communications, 1997). Filled with excellent, insightful grandparenting advice from an experienced family psychotherapist.

Totally Cool Grandparenting: A Practical Handbook of Tips, Hints, & Activities for the Modern Grandparent by Leslie Linsley (St. Martin's Press, 1997). Upfront advice, humor, and time-tested tactics, gathered from dozens of interviews with grandparents and grandkids.

Little Things Mean a Lot: Creating Happy Memories with Your Grandchildren by Susan Newman (Crown Publishers, 1996). Presents a creative sampling of simple ideas and projects to help grandparents pass on family traditions and develop a closer relationship with their grandchildren.

Contemporary Grandparenting by Arthur Kornhaber, M.D. (Sage Publications, 1996). A scholarly but readable and informative look at grandparenting.

Grandloving: Making Memories with Your Youngest Grandchildren by Sue Johnson and Julie Carlson (Heartstrings Press, 2003). An upbeat sourcebook on innovative and inexpensive activities for grandparents and grandchildren to do together.

Grandparents as Parents: A Survival Guide for Raising a Second Family by Sylvie de Toledo with Deborah Edler Brown (Guilford Press, 1995). A practical guide for grandparents raising grandchildren, from the founder of Grandparents as Parents support groups.

Children's Books That Feature Grandparents

The following books are appropriate for children from ages two through eight:

I Already Know I Love You by Billy Crystal (HarperCollins Children's Books, 2004). As a first-time grandfather, the comedian dreams of all the things he will do with his new grandchild.

Grandfather Counts by Andrea Cheng (Lee & Low, 2000). How a Chinese-speaking grandfather bonds with his English-speaking granddaughter by watching trains together.

Liliana's Grandmothers by Leyla Torres (Farrar, 1998). A look at Liliana's loving relationships with her white American grandmother who lives in Liliana's hometown and her other grandmother who lives in a Spanish-speaking country.

Mei-Mei Loves the Morning by Margaret Holloway Tsubakiyama (Whitman, 1999). Illustrated in beautiful watercolors, this book is a slice-of-life celebration of the loving relationship between Mei-Mei and her grandfather.

Coco Can't Wait by Taro Gomi (Viking, 1985). A story of a Japanese grandmother and granddaughter who can't wait to see each other.

When I Am Old with You by Angela Johnson (Orchard Books, 1993). A beautiful story of an African-American grandfather and grand-daughter and how they spend summer together.

A Kiss for Little Bear by Else Holmelund Minarik (Harper Trophy, 1984). The story of how a kiss between grandchild and grand-mother make for close friends among their friends.

Love You Forever by Robert Munsch (Firefly Books, 1995). The story of how a mother's love carries across two generations.

A Chair for My Mother by Vera Williams (Greenwillow, 1987). A grandmother helps her granddaughter save enough money for a chair for her mother, who works long hours.

Tell Me a Story, Mama by Angela Johnson (Orchard Books, 1992). An African-American mother tells her daughter stories of her own childhood with the child's grandparents and how the grandparents loved and raised her.

Something from Nothing by Phoebe Gilman (Scholastic Books, 1993). A beautiful Jewish folktale of a grandfather who makes a blanket for his grandson and what happens to the blanket in daily life in the shtetl where they live.

More, More, More by Vera Williams (Mulberry Books, 1996). A rich and affectionate story of how family members, including a grandmother, show their love for toddlers by playing with them.

Abuela by Arthur Dorros (Puffin, 1997, and Demco Media, 1997). A young girl takes a wonderful fanciful trip with her grandmother around Manhattan.

Thunder Cake by Patricia Polacco (Paper Star, 1997, and Demco Media, 1997). A grandmother helps her granddaughter with the child's fear of thunderstorms.

Annie and the Old One by Miska Miles (Little Brown, 1985, and Demco Media, 1985). A Native American girl comes to terms with her grandmother's eventual death through a beautiful weaving that her grandmother is working on.

Staying with Grandma by Eileen Roe (Simon & Schuster, 1989). A child's story about her visit to her grandmother's house in the country.

Stina and *Stina's Visit* by Lena Anderson (Greenwillow, 1989, and Greenwillow, 1991). Tender stories of a young Norwegian girl who spends summer vacations with her grandfather on a small coastal island of Norway.

The children's book list was prepared with the help of the Erikson Institute for the Advanced Study of Child Development. In several cases, the books were published in different formats by other publishers not listed here.